MW00805058

Media, Performative Identity, and the New
American Freak Show

Jessica L. Williams

# Media, Performative Identity, and the New American Freak Show

palgrave
macmillan

Jessica L. Williams
Department of English
SUNY College at Old Westbury
Westbury, NY, USA

ISBN 978-3-319-66461-3        ISBN 978-3-319-66462-0   (eBook)
DOI 10.1007/978-3-319-66462-0

Library of Congress Control Number: 2017950714

Cover image: © korionov/iStock/Getty Images Plus
Cover design by Henry Petrides

Printed on acid-free paper

This Palgrave Macmillan imprint is published by Springer Nature
The registered company is Springer International Publishing AG
The registered company address is: Gewerbestrasse 11, 6330 Cham, Switzerland

*For my girls*

# ACKNOWLEDGEMENTS

This book would not exist without the direction, support, and advice of my mentor, Scott Combs, a scholar whose knowledge, insight, and wit are staggering. The project began in the last year of my doctoral coursework, when Scott graciously agreed to work with me through an independent study on the freak show. The texts I studied that semester and the conversations we had about them have been the foundation for this book.

I'd also like to thank Derek Owens and Harry Denny from St. John's University. I've learned so much from both of you; thank you for your time, patience, and care. From SUNY Old Westbury, Margaret Torrell and Christopher Hobson have both been influential mentors who I can't thank enough. Your guidance and support over the years have been priceless. Thanks to all of my colleagues at Old Westbury, especially Danielle Lee for reading drafts of some later chapters and for being an all around great support.

Thank you to Glenn Ramirez and Shaun Vigil, both of whom have been tremendously helpul throughout the final stages of this project.

Thank you to my best friend, Corinne Lent who taught me to "surround yourself with people who believe in your dreams." My family is super rad and I love them all so much. Thank you to all of them but especially to my mom, without whom I never could have written this book, my brothers, Keith and Marc, my father, and my "Gma." My husband's family has been so supportive; thank you to all of them but especially to my mother-in-law, Kathy.

My husband, Dan, is the best person I know. My daughters are my everything. This book is for them.

Jessica L. Williams

# CONTENTS

# LIST OF FIGURES

## CHAPTER 1

# Introduction

On Thursday 14 February 2013, AMC premiered a new "unscripted" reality television show called *Freakshow* that chronicles the proprietor of the Venice Beach Freak Show, Todd Ray, his family, and the freak performers who perform at the show. Ray, a former music executive, collects and exhibits bizarre animals, such as his two-headed snake and two-headed dragon; novelty performers like Morgue, who inserts hooks, drills, metal balls, and other objects through various parts of his body; and physical anomalies such as Amazing Ali, who is three feet, five inches in height and George Bell who stands at seven feet, eight inches tall. Todd Ray talks often about the freak show and its traditions, narrating stories about famous freak performers, showing off his collection of freak show memorabilia, and otherwise painting the freak show and its history with pomp and pageantry.

Like all freak shows, the problem with *Freakshow* is not the people who perform in the show, but rather the way the freaks are exhibited. Todd Ray would have you believe that he is attempting to alter audience's perceptions with his freak show, or trying to eliminate the word "normal" from viewers' vocabularies. He sells himself as a collector of oddities, but comes across as exploitative and opportunistic. While he says, for instance, that he counts his freak performers as members of his

© The Author(s) 2017
J.L. Williams, *Media, Performative Identity, and the New American Freak Show*, DOI 10.1007/978-3-319-66462-0_1

family, the viewer cannot help but notice that the actual members of his family are physically normal,[1] or that he speaks about his human freaks the same way he does of his animal exhibits, collecting them both for his trophy case while claiming each as positive examples of freakishness.[2] Despite my criticisms, it is clear that Ray's *Freakshow* has tapped into a basic human desire—the satisfaction of curiosity—that has been fueling the presentation of freakish bodies for centuries. The difference here is that Ray's freak show occupies a dual space: it can be experienced live in person, a public sensationalized space; or in viewers' living rooms, a private domestic space.

*Freakshow* is more upfront in its attempt to reclaim the freak show than the films, documentaries, performers, and television shows that I examine in this book, but it is this reclamation that begins to thread all of my case studies together. While Ray claims to be bringing the freak show back to its roots, the very fact that the viewer is watching it on television makes it a different entity than the traditional freak show. The many examples I take up throughout my discussion are marked by similar transitions. This project is concerned with representations of freak bodies, which is something different to the bodies themselves. In other words, the bodies being discussed in these pages have been mediated, like *Freakshow*, before they reach the viewer. While the original freak show body was itself mediated through costuming, back stories, and other means of exaggeration, the freak bodies that audiences see today have been mediated even further. I write about the relationship between

---

[1] His family all work at the Venice Beach Freak Show with him, although, with the exception of his daughter, none of them are performers. Asia, his daughter, is actually quite attractive and only becomes a "freak" performer when she is taught sword swallowing by one of the show's freaks. In this episode, she appears to learn how to swallow swords in a matter of a few days, becoming the world's youngest female sword swallower.

[2] Another example of Ray's ambiguous motives comes when he tries to fix the relationship between Creature, a heavily tattooed and pierced African American man in his show, and his young daughter who fears him. In this segment, Ray becomes a modern-day Prospero, a colonist taming a monster. Although Ray tries to paint himself as Creature's equal in this scene, Creature's embodiment of a Caliban-esque monster capable of harming a child (Creature's daughter fears his appearance as Miranda feared Caliban because of his attempted rape of her) and Ray's positioning as the white ruler suggest that the relationship between the two men is not one of equality but of unbalanced power that bears the threat of colonization.

normal and freakish bodies through different media because changing media has altered the relationship between these bodies.

## THE MEDIATED FREAK: CLOSENESS AND FARNESS

I am concerned with the way freak bodies are represented in various media and what those representations reveal about the viewer's relationship with the freakish body. The representations that I explore raise questions about representation and authenticity exactly because they mediate the viewer's relationship—both temporally and spatially—to the freak body. Ultimately, the freak show is not just being appropriated through media but the relationship to the freak body is itself becoming disseminated. Because the viewer-object or freak-norm relationship becomes blurred when freak and non-freak bodies collide, the space of consumption becomes a freak show mediated by modes of entertainment.

All of the images (from photographs, film, television, music videos, and the internet) that I will be discussing have been filtered through a lens, which always involves a level of subjectivity: someone chooses the subject, takes and edits the images, and otherwise personalizes the images before they reach the viewer. In *Practices of Looking*, Marita Sturken and Lisa Cartwright examine the subjectivity of mediated imagery and how images are connected to systems of power. Here, they tell us that despite the high level of subjective involvement in the production of images, "the aura of machine objectivity clings to mechanical and electronic images" (16). Photographs, for example, can be seen as scientific tools for registering data. They are often seen as "unmediated cop[ies] of the real world, a trace of reality skimmed off the very surface of life" (17). This "myth of photographic truth" allows the viewer to see the freak body through the objective eye of the camera, and thus register the image in a way more "real" or "true" than the human eye can. However, it is essential to recognize that images, because they are representations of reality and not reality itself, "are produced within dynamics of social power and ideology" (21). The term "representation" refers to the "use of language and images to create meaning about the world around us" (12). Audiences utilize words and images to explain and understand the world, and do this through "systems of representation" such as photography, television, and film. It is through these systems of representation, rather than the material world, that viewers "actually construct the meaning of the material world" (12–13). Sturken clarifies this further when she says that "[l]anguage and systems of representation do not reflect an already existing reality so much as they organize, construct, and mediate our understanding of reality, emotion, and imagination" (13). The illusion of reality clouds the fact that mediated images often reinforce hegemonic values and ideologies such as "the value of romantic love, the norm of heterosexuality, nationalism, or traditional concepts of good and evil" (21). These ideologies often appear natural or inherent, but are actually learned concepts reinforced by a culture of mediated images that have the power to influence the viewing public. Ultimately, this give and take between media and reality results in a conflation of the two concepts: media representations are our reality.

Unlike media representations, the traditional live freak show required a face-to-face confrontation between freak and viewer. Therefore, each show, despite the repetitiveness of the acts, was a one-of-a-kind experience, unable to be perfectly reproduced. Rachel Adams picks up on this in *Sideshow U.S.A.*, noting that "[u]nlike media transmitted through mechanical reproduction, human exhibits provide opportunities for unanticipated exchanges between customers and freaks" (29). Many would argue that the physical and temporal separation of viewers and freaks eliminates any possibility of true interaction between the two. Despite this separation, the media that has taken the place of the freak show—film and television, specifically—still allow for a relationship between object and viewer, freak and norm.[3] This relationship, built on both distance and intimacy, farness and closeness, will be a focus throughout the book because it reveals the cultural organization of different bodies.

With the disappearance of the live freak show, freaks pass "inevitably from the platform and the pit to the screen, flesh becoming shadow" (Fiedler 16). Leslie Fiedler feels that "the loss of the old confrontation in the flesh implies a trauma" that is "irreparable" (16). He believes that the obsolescence of the old freak show is itself a trauma that cannot be undone or replaced by appropriations of the freak body. Similarly, Thomas Fahy believes that as the distance between normal and other bodies collapsed throughout American society, the freak show no longer

---

[3] "Norm," short for "normal," is a term I will use interchangeably with "able-bodied" throughout. I like the harshness of the term "norm," especially when paired with the brusque term "freak".

worked in allowing people to lessen their anxieties about normalcy (4). The freak show succeeded, according to Fahy, because it reinforced binaries about gender, race, and ability but its failure was cemented when scientific advances and human rights issues altered the ways viewers saw otherness. Like Fiedler, Fahy relegates the freak show to irrelevance and obscurity, citing the lack of a cultural need for it. I disagree with these assessments because what Fahy and Fiedler, among others, fail to take into consideration is that the binaries once challenged by the freak show still exist and are still being challenged and explored by the entertainment institutions that have replaced the freak show. While audiences may have lost the physical closeness of the freak-norm encounter with the disappearance of the live freak show, I believe we have gained an emotional, cultural closeness with the portrayals that have taken its place.

The "new American freak show" is characterized by the ways that moving image media transmits and contextualizes the freak body. There has been a gradual closing of the gap between viewers and freakish bodies on screens. The traditional freak show had gone out of favor with the general public by the dawn of cinema's Golden Age. The movement of the freak body from the freak show to the film screen was significant because of the striking spatial and temporal distance that now existed between viewers and the bodies being viewed. This distancing helps to create the illusion that what is being watched onscreen is fictitious, even if it resembles the viewers' reality. Despite whatever horror is found onscreen, the actual bodies of viewers remained distanced from the bodies being viewed. Television then took a step forward in removing the screen between freak and norm. Watching the freak body on a television screen makes the freak body more intimate because of its presence in the home of the viewer, and the fictitiousness of the freak body is lessened further with "real-life" depictions of freak bodies on viewers' television screens. However, the freak body is still, of course, distanced in space and time and so remains largely innocuous to the viewer. In a final shift in removing the gap between freak and viewer, popular performers, who are often self-made freaks, and of the celebrity culture that breeds cultural freakishness, have made the screen between freak and viewer impermanent. Celebrity culture, specifically within the music industry, transcends the limits of media: audiences see their bodies on the internet, television, film, print, onstage, and in the streets. Their freakishness can be kept at a distance but it isn't always. As in Todd Ray's *Freakshow*, viewers can see their bodies in the flesh, can physically touch their bodies, and can come face-to-face with freak culture. In addition, the bodies of viewers are often altered as a result of their contact with the freak, especially in the cases of disability porn and performers like Marilyn Manson and Lady Gaga. These interactions, of course, change the relationship between freak and norm because they place freakishness back into the real world of the viewer.

Thus the visual culture that has emerged since the freak show's marginalization takes the place of the traditional freak show but also opens new channels of interpretation and identification through its use of mediated images as well as the altered freak-norm relationship that it has fostered. These new freak representations introduce narratives about sex, gender, and cultural perceptions of people with disabilities and, because they highlight the ways in which the freak body is situated as a broken, pitiable, sexless, monstrous, dangerous, impotent, feminized, or otherwise *undesirable* body, many of these representations still clearly have work to do.

The spectacle of the freak body is an objectified reality that has been inscribed meaning both by those who construct it and by those who consume it through media. The representations of freak bodies that I explore in the following chapters are realities that have been constructed of images, presented as spectacle, and consumed by a collective viewer who would inscribe meaning onto those bodies.

## FREAK AS PERFORMATIVE IDENTITY

Robert Bogdan tells us that the freak show has been referred to by many names: Raree Show, Hall of Human Curiosities, Sideshow, 10-in-1, Kid Show, Pit Show, Odditorium, Congress of Oddities, Congress of Human Wonders, Museum of Nature's Mistakes, and Freak Show, as well as numerous variations of these (3). I choose to call the presentation of human oddities for money, and the people who are presented, by the names "freak show" and "freaks," respectively and respectfully. To some, it may be jarring to hear a person with disabilities or anomalies referred to as a freak, or their performances a freak show. To clarify, when I use the term "disabled" throughout this book, I am referring to a cultural perception of disability. In other words, while it may be true that certain people with physical limitations may not consider themselves disabled, the large majority of general society would. So, when I say "person with disabilities," "disability," or "anomaly," I am referring to physical deviations from what is socialized as a "normal" and "healthy" body. My use of the term "freak" to describe such bodies seems appropriate to me in the sense that I am using the language of the freak show, a language in which the term freak is not derogatory. Freak, as I use it, does not refer to the entire population of people with disabilities, but rather those who have publically displayed their bodies (or have had their bodies put on display) for purposes of entertainment, art, or profit. Thus, while this book largely focuses on the bodies of people with disabilities (or appropriations of those bodies), I also refer to the female body and the non-white body as freakish throughout. In these cases, the same logic applies: they are freakish in the way that are being visually represented to the viewer.

Actually, the medical term for a person born with visible physical deformities or disabilities from the Middle Ages was not freak but "monster." Although the etymology of the word is unclear, it either stems from "*moneo*, meaning to warn, or *monstro*, meaning to show forth" (Fiedler 20). Many of our current ideas about freakish bodies come from Middle Age and Renaissance notions of monstrosity and spectacle. Philosopher and theorist Mikhail Bakhtin's *Rabelais and his World*, a rich examination of humor and carnival culture during the Middle Ages and the Renaissance, provides crucial insight in understanding the origins of the carnivalesque and will be significant throughout this discussion. Bakhtin tells us that the carnival—the experience of it but also the grotesque body—was characterized by its undefined forms and impermanence. He calls this "the peculiar logic of the 'inside out,' of the 'turnabout,' of a continual shifting from top to bottom, from front to rear, of numerous parodies and travesties, humiliations, profanations, comic crownings and uncrownings" (11). This "peculiar logic," in part, defines the anomalous body; it too is marked by a continual shifting, being inside out, upside down, exaggerated, or otherwise out of place. Bakhtin says that images of the grotesque body in Rabelais and other Renaissance literature are marked by their portrayal of the body as universal and deeply connected to the earth. The body is not individualized but is a collective, earthly body that cannot be separated from the earth; this is why "all that is bodily becomes grandiose, exaggerated, immeasurable." The grotesque body is one of "fertility, life, and a brimming-over abundance" but also one of degradation, "the lowering of all that is high, spiritual, ideal, abstract" (18–19).

These descriptions certainly bring to mind the bodies of the freak show. Often seeming exaggerated and possessing either "too much" or "too little" body, freak bodies are, like the monstrous bodies in horror that I will discuss in Chap. 3, characterized by ambivalence and contradiction. Missing or extra limbs, the presence of hair where there should be none, a disproportionate body, or otherwise aesthetically unpleasing bodies fit Bakhtin's description of the grotesque body in that they are "contrary to the classic images of the finished, completed man, cleansed, as it were, of all the scoriae of birth and development" (25). The disabled, deformed, or otherwise anomalous body was, therefore, seen as monstrous because it appeared in some way unfinished, "transgress[ing] its own limits" (Bakhtin 26).

By the eighteenth century, monster went out of favor for a term that P.T. Barnum popularized in referring to his exhibits: curiosities.[4] In addition to anomalous and disabled bodies, Barnum's curiosities included attractions which would not have been considered monsters, but something quite different. Examples include the Woolly Horse and Jumbo the Elephant, as well as exhibits discussed more fully in the next chapter, Joice Heth, said to be George Washington's 161-year-old nurse, and the Feejee Mermaid (Fiedler 15). As the differences between "monster" and "curiosity" highlight, there is more than one category of freak. Monsters, also known as *lusus naturae* or freaks of nature, were only one type of human exhibit. Also common was the exhibition of new and unknown races, popular because of the exploration of the non-Western world in the eighteenth and nineteenth centuries. Freaks of gender were both natural and gaffed: bearded ladies and half-men/half-women could be easily faked if real gender freaks could not be found. Finally, there was the novelty act, including performers such as sword swallowers, snake charmers, and heavily pierced and tattooed men and women. By the last quarter of the nineteenth century, the categories of human exhibition—monsters, racial freaks, and novelty acts—were all considered, simply, freaks (Bogdan 7).

Most relevant scholarship makes a distinction between the freak of nature and the freak of culture, the former being a person born with

---

[4]By "exhibit" I specifically refer to freak show curiosities who were displayed and viewed for profit. Not all freak exhibits were human; pickled punks (real or imitation human fetuses or animals with anatomical anomalies which were preserved in jars) and taxidermy animals were also popular freak show exhibits.

their freakishness, or having obtained it through some accident or misfortune (disability, deformity), and the latter having intentionally created their freakishness (racial freaks,[5] novelty acts). However, in the context of this study, these distinctions are not of primary concern, though, when relevant, I do discuss the differences. In fact, the concept of freak as a performative identity is not a new one and it is one that is noted in most studies. To me, this seems to supersede any conversation about nature/nurture because, in this approach, all freaks are freaks of culture.

Therefore it is significant to understand that the quality of freakishness depends very much on social and historical context. Heavily tattooed men and women, for example, were certainly considered freaks in early American sideshows, and are now a fairly common and accepted sight in American society. With few exceptions, the stories told to audience members about the lives of freaks were fictitious or, at the very least, quite exaggerated versions of the truth. Although viewers want to interpret or take meaning from freakish bodies, these anomalies are not in themselves what make a person a freak. As Bogdan notes: "The onstage freak is something else offstage. 'Freak' is a frame of mind, a set of practices, a way of thinking about and presenting people" (xi). Many exhibits actually had a large hand in creating their own freak personas. Bogdan offers an interesting example with the story of Jack Earle:

> In the 1920s when Clyde Ingalls asked Jack Earle, the tall Texan, whether he wanted to be a giant, he was inviting him to join a well-established institution. Jack needed the freak show to become a giant. Not only did it supply the platform and the audience, but it provided the idea of "freak" and the patterns to construct an exhibit as well. While each freak had to be made separately, and each had a unique stamp, the freak show had developed the flexible mold, the instructions, and the perspective by which the exhibit could be constructed. (25)

Bogdan is illustrating that freak is a performative identity that requires a spectacular narrative and an audience in order to exist. Earle was not a giant before joining the freak show—he was simply a tall man. Neither is his identity transformed to freak in stepping foot onto the stage; rather, freak is the identity Earle performs once there. But he cannot take on the

---

[5] Though a racial freak is, of course, born into their race, their freakishness is constructed through costuming and fictional narratives.

persona of freak himself; he needs the viewer to complete his identity as freak. As viewers, "our reaction to freaks is ... the result of our socialization, and of the way our social institutions managed these people's identities. Freak shows are ... about organizations and patterned relationships between them and us" (Bogdan xi). This relationship—them and us— will be a central focus throughout this book.

## CHAPTER OVERVIEWS

In Chap. 2, "A New American Freak Show," I provide a historical framework for the rest of the book by tracing the history of the freak show in Europe and America, focusing on the latter, from antiquity through its decline in the early twentieth century. The rest of the chapter develops a theoretical framework that includes a discussion about the viewer's relationship to the freak show, and how and why we look at unusual bodies. Because this project exists at the intersection of many different areas, including cultural studies, film and media studies, and gender and disability, I aim to provide only the key terms and concepts from each area that are immediately relevant to my argument.

Each of the chapters that follows focuses on a different mediation in popular entertainment through which to contextualize the freakish body. The third chapter, "Horror Movies, Horror Bodies: Blurring the Freak Body in Cinema," examines the disabled body as a sight of spectacle and identification in film through a lengthy discussion of Tod Browning's 1932 film *Freaks*. I have chosen this discussion to frame the chapter because *Freaks* has been used by critics as a lens through which to understand the freak show itself. This is problematic because a film, and the history it attempts to portray are, of course, not one and the same. However, *Freaks* serves as an example of how film has *interpreted* the freak show and the freak body and has provided a groundwork for both creating and understanding future melodramas and horror films. I also examine horror staples *Rosemary's Baby* and *The Texas Chainsaw Massacre*, as well as *The Funhouse*, which shares the same director as the latter, and the melodrama *The Elephant Man*. Each discussion unpacks the human monsters who exist at the center of the films, how the monstrous body is portrayed, and how these films work either in or against the tradition of the freak show. Ultimately, I argue that the freak show exists in horror when normal and freakish bodies collide.

Chapter 4, "Reality, Normality, Sexuality: 'Authentic' Portrayals of the Freak," argues that "real-life" portrayals of the freak body such as reality television and documentaries attempt to recreate the freak show through allowing the viewer to experience the freak body in an uncensored and unmonitored way, thus enabling viewers to experience the intimacy of freak bodies by providing access to their daily lives. Specifically, I look at TLC's lineup of body-obsessed reality shows and documentaries, the documentary *Murderball* and The Sundance Channel's docudrama *Push Girls* as examples of mediated real-life representations of the freak body. Ultimately, I find that the mode of presentation is significant in the access it gives the viewer to the freak body, as well as in its contact with freak sexuality. Both regulate how much and what kind of access the viewer has to the "real" freak body, and because these are reality-based portrayals, they offer commentaries on current attitudes toward gender and sexuality as it pertains to the freak body.

Chapter 5 bridges the gap between my discussions of "safe" freak sexuality in *Push Girls* and *Murderball* in Chap. 4, and my deliberations about the dissemination of the freak show in the last chapter by examining explicit depictions of disabled sexuality via disability pornography and the documentary *Sick: The Life and Death of Bob Flanagan Supermasochist*. My sixth and final chapter, "Born This Way? Pop Culture's Collision with the Freak of Nature," discusses culturally constructed freakishness in the representations of the freak body in popular music's visual culture. I look at the music videos and live performances of shock rocker Marilyn Manson and pop star Lady Gaga to argue that physical ability, sexuality, and gender identities help shape cultural constructions of freakishness and therefore cannot be separated from freakish bodies. My examinations of Manson and Gaga reveal the hierarchy that exists within categories of freakishness and how, as the made freak body comes into contact with the born freak body, it is revealed as being inauthentic. Ultimately, however, this inauthenticity doesn't matter in the pop culture sphere because when the freak is disseminated through changing media, the separation because normal and freakish bodies, and therefore the distance between freak show and everyday life, collapses; the freak show is dispersed.

## CHAPTER 2

# A New American Freak Show

Human beings born with physical anomalies have always been treated as exceptions. As Elizabeth DePoy and Stephen French Gilson note: "As early as ancient civilizations, there is documentation of a range of responses to 'the atypical human' from fascination to revulsion" (9). While many cultures have revered those with physical differences, such as the Ancient Egyptians who worshiped and mummified them, most societies cast out or killed such people, such as the ancient Greeks and Romans who ritually killed people with disabilities and deformities. Despite the range in treatment of people with physical anomalies, history reveals some commonalities, notably that what is considered atypical varies depending on time, location, and context; explanations for atypical bodies are widely varied and conflicting; and these explanations not only reveal the "beliefs, values, politics, economics, intellectual trends, and level of technological development of the times," but they have also shaped how we categorize and view such bodies today (9–10).

For many, including medieval Christians, such "anomalous births" were explained through teleological reasoning. Three common rationales were generally given by Christians for the existence of anomalous bodies: "as signs of God's wrath, occasioned by sin; as a reminder that each birth was as miraculous as the original Creation; and as omens and portents, intended for our good" (Fiedler 230). These teleological reasons explained the existence of human "monsters" in terms of the purpose their existences ultimately served. Therefore, many medieval Christians felt that they must accept human oddities and the reasons behind their

© The Author(s) 2017
J.L. Williams, *Media, Performative Identity, and the New American Freak Show*, DOI 10.1007/978-3-319-66462-0_2

13

existence. Many were killed anyway, accused of being products of witch-craft, and hence killed as part of God's work. Religious texts including "the Hebrew Bible, early Christian and Muslim documents, and [various religious] images of the times" are rich with literal and symbolic references to "atypical human conditions, appearances, and behaviors" (DePoy and Gilson 14). Islam and the Hebrews shared a particular disdain for those with anomalies, casting out or otherwise marginalizing people with disabilities, while Jewish texts show that those with anomalies were thought to be punished by God but were not excluded from communities or religious services (14).

While there is much disagreement among historians and scholars over accounts of disability during the Middle Ages, it seems clear that despite the prominence of the church, and its theological rationales that saw people with abnormalities as everything "from monster to miracle," Western Europe during the Middle Ages was the starting point for the medicalization of disability and the thinking that disabled bodies could and ought to be treated and cured if possible. The Middle Ages also saw the rise of both the institutional and charity models of disability, which placed people with disabilities as patients or persons in need of pity and charity (16).

By the beginning of the seventeenth century, views about physical difference were being significantly altered. In America, the view of human oddities as either "tokens of the Lord's vengeance or as instruments of the devil" was particularly powerful throughout the seventeenth century, and reached a peak with the Salem witch trials in the 1690s (Fiedler 230–231). However, the Enlightenment in Europe and the New World largely saw supernatural beliefs overthrown by science, and such scientific advances added to the increasing sense that the anomalous body "could be explained by observations in the physical world" (231). DePoy and Gilson acknowledge authors and artists such as Leonardo Da Vinci and Francis Bacon for contributing to the belief in separation between mind and body that saw the mind "characterized as logical and triumphant over and controlling of the flesh" thus "locating disability within the weakened body [and] opening it up for scrutiny and cure" (18). Disabled bodies, therefore, suggested not only a weakened body but a weakened mind as well. This thinking further marked the disabled body as a site for medical analysis.

Another significant change during the Enlightenment is the distinction made between deformities at birth and those acquired later in life.

Now carrying value distinctions, disabilities were ranked according to how they were acquired. DePoy and Gilson offer an example: "some birth-based failures in activities for typical growth were explained as 'monstrosities,' while differences in what individuals did that resulted from observable explanations, such as injury, were regarded as natural" (18–19). Finally, disability became associated with poverty during this era, in part, because the number of those with physical illnesses and abnormalities was disproportionately larger than those who appeared normal and in good health (19–20).

As this brief history shows, abnormal bodies have been scrutinized for meaning, social significance, and cultural value, and have been mostly negatively viewed, only accepted begrudgingly, for centuries.[1] Like the exceptional treatment of people with anomalies, the exhibition of human oddities has existed from antiquity, though they were first displayed for entertainment purposes in Europe during the Middle Ages. For many years, human oddities were displayed by their families in their own homes, or in private exhibitions at royal courts. Later, they were exhibited in groups to the general population, though only as omens from the Church. During the Elizabethan era, the public exhibition of freaks was first recorded, but it was not until the Restoration that they first became "stellar attractions" (Fiedler 279–280).

## Bakhtin, Barnum, and the Exhibition of Human Oddities

Folk culture, including art, theater, and carnival, during the Middle Ages and the Renaissance in Europe, saw the spectacular body in practically the same way they did other sources of entertainment—with humor. Mikhail Bakhtin characterizes this humor as implicit to carnival, saying that "[i]n spite of their variety, folk festivities of the carnival type, the comic rites and cults, the clowns and fools, giants, dwarfs, and jugglers, the vast and manifold literature of parody—all these forms have one style in common: they belong to the culture of folk carnival humor" (4). Bakhtin's examination of Renaissance literature offers terrific insight into

---

[1] This is an extremely reductive retelling of a rich body of work concerned with disability throughout history. For an incomparably more thorough account, see the chapter "Looking Back" in *Studying Disability* by DePoy and Gilson, as well as *A History of Disability* by Henri-Jacques Striker, and even Leslie Fiedler's "From Theology to Teratology" in *Freaks: Myths and Images of the Secret Self.*

the way the body was once viewed, and it helps provide a framework for the way we currently read anomalous bodies.

Bakhtin tells us that carnival festivities, which included spectacles such as those noted above, were an important part of medieval life:

> Besides carnivals proper, with their long and complex pageants and processions, there was the 'feast of fools' and the 'feast of the ass'; there was a special free 'Easter laughter,' consecrated by tradition. Moreover, nearly every church feast had its comic folk aspect, which was also traditionally recognized. Such, for instance, were the parish feasts, usually marked by fairs and varied open-air amusements, with the participation of giants, dwarfs, monsters, and trained animals. ... [There were] agricultural feasts as the harvesting of the grapes which was celebrated also in the city. Civil and social ceremonies and rituals such as the tribute rendered to the victors at tournaments, the transfer of feudal rights, or the initiation of a knight. (5)

Such events were non-official and non-political forms of entertainment and celebration, but to ignore them would be to miss a large and important aspect of the culture of the Middle Ages and the Renaissance. These carnivals and their treatment of human spectacle suggest a unique moment in the relationship between viewer and freak. Here, the relationship to the freak body is lighthearted and celebratory; the freak body is something to laugh rather than scream at or shy away from.

The significance of this is underscored as Bakhtin clarifies that although carnival and its imagery resemble artistic forms, specifically the spectacle, carnival should not be mistaken for art. Rather, Bakhtin contends that carnival "belongs to the borderline between art and life." He adds that carnival was, in fact, "life itself, but shaped according to a certain pattern of play" and, further, that "carnival does not know footlights, in the sense that it does not acknowledge any distinction between actors and spectators" (6–7). The lines between performance and real life are blurred. Further, Bakhtin suggests that what happens in carnival is merely life performed, and that spectators felt no distinction between their lives and the spectacle before them. Fools, clowns, actors, giants, and other spectacles did not "act" onstage; they were the same wherever and whenever they went, standing "on the borderline between life and art" (8). Bakhtin's concepts of the body and the grotesque are crucial in understanding the presentation and definition of the freak body because, although viewers have spent roughly two to three centuries treating the freak body with horror, disgust, and fear, I believe the new American freak show is characterized by a slight return to Bakhtin's notion of the freak body.

The American freak show began in the mid-eighteenth century. Following the lead of the English Renaissance Fairs discussed here by Bakhtin, human curiosities were traveling exhibits with "managers or showmen who did the promoting, made the business arrangements, and collected the admission charge" (Bogdan 25). Traveling animal exhibits were just as popular as human ones, if not more, at this time; both were referred to collectively as "living curiosities." Both human and animal oddities were unusual and unfamiliar to audiences who had never seen such a thing as a giraffe or a little person and, because science was not a developed field at the time, viewers "might very well believe that [oddities] were from the moon, or from the dark crevices of one of the mysterious landmasses not yet penetrated by Westerners." By the nineteenth century, Americans were captivated by freak show oddities who now saw freak bodies as "a part of God's great order of creatures" and who were therefore "subject to scientific study and classification." Scientific interest in *lusus naturae*, or human monsters, justified and reinforced the public's interest in such bodies (Bogdan 25–28).

Around 1840, the freak show was institutionalized. This means that freak shows moved from being unattached attractions—"single attractions that were not attached to organizations such as circuses and carnivals"—to an integral part of American entertainment (Bogdan 11). When independent and traveling oddities became more permanently housed in museums, they were able to develop, for the first time, a "community [and] culture of showpeople" (30). This permanence afforded freak performers the opportunity to become part of a larger collective—"the freak show"—rather than relying on a single manager or a small unincorporated traveling troupe (30).

Perhaps the single most important event in the institutionalization of the freak show was when Phineas Taylor Barnum established his American Museum in New York City in 1841. Barnum was the first to recognize the potential of the freak show to become a commercial success. In fact, it was only in the 1840s that the term "freak" came to be used in reference to the exhibition of people with anomalies. As Thomas Fahy notes, this is significant because it suggests a change in the presentation of freak bodies at this particular time, and that change—the institutionalization of the freak show—was brought about largely by P.T. Barnum (7). Rachel Adams points out that "Barnum was responsible for transforming the freak show into a coordinated business venture enhanced by advertising, promotional materials, and celebrity appearances." Barnum's American Museum—a combination of theater, carnival, lecture, and freak show—became the model for the American freak show institution, where audiences paid one price to see a variety of freak exhibits—hence one of the freak show's many alternate monikers, the 10-in-1 (Adams 11).

In his zeal to be the most successful and most shocking businessman in entertainment, Barnum and his American Museum developed a reputation and set a precedent for the types of exhibits seen at freak shows. The American Museum saw a larger variety of acts than any other venue of its kind due to Barnum's diligent searching of the country for "industrious fleas, automatons, jugglers, ventriloquists, living statuary, tableaux, gypsies, albinos, fat boys, giants, dwarfs, rope-dancers, dioramas, panoramas, models of Niagara, Dublin, Paris and Jerusalem...Punch and Judy...fancy glass-blowing, knitting machines...dissolving views, American Indians" and anything else that might bring paying customers off the streets and into the building (Harris qt. Barnum 40–41). He made sure to show his exhibits on a rotating basis in order to keep them novel and exciting. His biggest hits, however, included the mainstays Joice Heth, "George Washington's nurse"; General Tom Thumb; and the Feejee Mermaid.

Joice Heth, a former slave who claimed to be 161-years-old and the former nurse of George Washington, was one of Barnum's first real successes. Appealing because of her patriotic story and exoticism, Heth was promoted by Barnum with great extravagance and success. However, after many shows and tours with Heth, her popularity began to wane. This led to one of Barnum's most infamous stunts: he wrote an animated letter and sent it anonymously to a local newspaper claiming outrage at the fraudulent exhibit. This bit of anti-hype rejuvenated interest in Heth and made Barnum and his oddity even more successful than before (Harris 21–23). Another infamous attraction, Tom Thumb, whose real name was Charles S. Stratton, was a midget who, when Barnum met him, was five-years-old, just over two feet tall, and a mere 15 lb in weight. Adorned with miniature "ponies, uniforms, and carriages," he was, as Neil Harris describes him, the "perfect man-child," someone with whom crowds could identify and enjoy (43, 49).

Considered Barnum's "most famous put-on of all," the Feejee Mermaid was an oddity purchased by Barnum that had "the body of a fish and the head and hands of a monkey." A back story was created, claiming that the mermaid was discovered in Fiji by the distinguished "Dr. Griffin," really the man who had been hired to manage the exhibit (Harris 62–63). While many audience members readily believed Barnum's claims about the mermaid, it was actually the torso and head of a baby monkey sewn to the back half of a fish and covered in papier-mâché.

Barnum's great success was born out of his related talents in advertising and deceiving audiences. Harris tells us that from the start of Barnum's career in entertainment, "carting about the fabled Joice Heth," he was completely "aware of his ability to gull others, to make them pay for the opportunity of being fooled" (Harris 57). As Harris implies here, the audiences were perfectly aware of Barnum's early and lasting reputation for "humbuggery" and knew that they might not see what Barnum's advertisements promised. In fact, audiences often delighted at finding that they'd been tricked and enjoyed "the competition between victim and hoaxer" (77). Much of Barnum's success resulted from taking advantage of people's desire for truth; audiences yearned to know whether or not an exhibit was authentic. They even paid Barnum in addition to the attraction price for access to his "ticket-seller's analysis" which would explain how the "humbugs" were successfully achieved. The desire to discover an exhibit's authenticity remains a fascinating truth of current freak bodies and performances.

In many ways, Barnum and exhibits such as these became standards of the American freak show. When the American Museum burned down in 1868, Barnum retired from the industry, but his museum became the prototype for dime museums which were popular from around 1870 to 1900. Dime museums were exactly what they sound like: museums that cost a dime for admission. These were popular throughout the USA, though New York claimed the most museums and best attractions. Freak performers were the featured attractions of these museums although, as Bogdan tells us,

> Museum managers, under increased competition not only from other museums but from circus sideshows and other amusement organizations, often promoted the shabbiest of human oddities and gaffed freaks as scientific sensations and singular attractions. Following the lead of earlier freak

promoters, most notably P.T. Barnum, they raised fraud, misrepresentation, and exaggeration—the hard sell—to new heights. (35–37)

To clarify, during this time freak shows were attached to these small
dime museums as well as circuses, world's fairs, amusement parks, and
carnivals. Although the freak show was attached to larger organizations
which were all fairly different, they shared a similar culture and most
freak shows were formatted similarly: barkers and spectacular banners
and advertisements drew in crowds; spectators often had to look up on
a stage or down into a pit to see the freak performers; placards and postcards told exaggerated or fictional narratives about the freaks onstage;
and crowds were lured into a final "blow-off" for an extra cost.

Mainstays of the freak show included people with disabilities, deformities, or other physical differences; characters who were physically normal
but who were costumed and performed created narratives; and novelty
acts. Very tall or short, and very fat and thin people were often paired
together or with average-sized people, or dressed in ways to exaggerate their size. Exotic peoples from distant lands were costumed as barbaric wild men and women, or as perfect "Circassian" beauties of fine
Caucasian stock. Novelty acts included tattooed people, flame throwers,
snake charmers, and sword swallowers (they were also often "exotic"
performers). Gender-bending acts such as the half-man/half-woman and
the Bearded Lady were very popular freak show staples, but perhaps the
most popular exhibits were those with disabilities. People missing limbs,
conjoined twins, people with bizarre growths and deformities, and people with peculiar conditions, such as the infamous Dog-Faced Boy who
grew hair all over his face, were popular because of their rarity.

From approximately 1840 to 1940, the freak show was a part of
American entertainment whose popularity was undeniable. Throughout
the nineteenth century, the exhibition of humans in freak shows was
appreciated by most walks of life. Doctors and scientists were particularly drawn to human anomalies because of their rarity and usefulness as
objects of medical and scientific inquiry (Bogdan 27). Even the upper
crust found the freak show to be an acceptable form of entertainment;
many even collected freak show souvenir cards, commonly referred to as
*cartes de visite*,[2] and displayed them in albums in their homes.

---

[2] See note 6.

## THE DECLINE OF THE FREAK SHOW

The turn of the century, however, saw a changing attitude toward freak shows which can be credited to a number of factors. Many would agree with Leslie Fiedler's assertion that the freak show's popularity dropped off steadily at the end of the Victorian age due to "Victorian sentimentality and morality," which suggests that because of the rigid moral views held by many people of the time, the display of anomalous bodies for entertainment purposes would have been deemed to be both in poor taste and immoral (Fiedler 16). Robert Bogdan, however, offers a more matter-of-fact explanation by claiming that it was the freak show's own popularity that was, in large part, its undoing. He tells us that there was such a large demand for freak exhibits and such a shortage of people with strange enough anomalies that promoters went on "freak hunts" to find exhibits for their shows. This "freak shortage" resulted in a surplus of "[n]ovelty acts, non-Western exotics, self-made freaks, and gaffs" to fill in, the result of which was that "bizarre hyperbole dominated" (Bogdan 37). Freak shows became places to be ripped off, rather than to see someone truly spectacular, and most of the crowds stopped showing up, leaving the freak shows to "immigrants and country bumpkins" (38). The lack of interesting exhibits, of course, contributed to the view of the freak show as an undesirable and, frankly, unsuccessful form of entertainment.

Also significant is that, at the turn of the century, Mendel's laws of genetics were rediscovered and applied to human traits. Bogdan writes,

> This new perspective was accompanied by the rise of the eugenics movement, a vicious use of social Darwinism which cautioned the nation that because modern societies protected their weak, the principle of survival of the fittest was not working. The weak, the imperfect, the social, mental, and physical misfits, they warned, would, if left unchecked, breed at such a rate as to outnumber the better breeding stock. (62)

Now that "physically and mentally inferior people" were seen as a danger, they were largely separated from society by being placed into asylums and hospitals. Bogdan also cites the continued exploration of other parts of the world as a reason for the freak show's loss of favor in America. This was especially important in terms of displaying non-whites in the freak show. The racial freak, also known as the ethnographic freak, has a fascinating and tragic history. Rachel Adams provides two excellent examples in her case studies of Ota Benga, an "African Savage" who was displayed in the Monkey House at the Bronx Zoo in 1906, and Ishi, "The Last Wild Indian," a freak show performer who was advertised in 1911 as being "the last of his kind" (31–59). Adams' examples depict individuals with clear ethnographic identities which were used as a point of spectacle. Narratives were created around their identities in order to draw curious and often horrified spectators. Logically, as Americans learned more about the world and the many different types of people in it, they were much more skeptical when being spun a tale about "the myths and legends of lost tribes of giants and pygmies and natives with tails" (Bogdan 63). The more people learned about the world, in other words, the harder it was to offer them a mystical, otherworldly experience at the freak show.

The medical field was learning much more as well: "Like the freak show, physicians had become organized and by 1900 were well on their way to professionalizing" (Bogdan 63). In doing so, they also became authorities on large numbers of human afflictions: "Human differences became medicalized as pathological—as 'disease'" (63). Following these changes, the scientific community launched an attack on the freak show; they implied that freaks should not be exhibited, but rather should be treated under the care of a doctor, and were "to be viewed on hospital rounds and in private offices, by appointment only" (64). Bogdan cites an article from a 1908 issue of *Scientific Weekly*, "Circus and Museum Freaks, Curiosities of Pathology," that harshly criticized the exhibition of people whom the author refers to as "humble and unfortunate individuals" to a "gaping and unsympathetic crowd" (64). This article is the first "assault" on the freak show by the medical profession and sent the strong message that the freak bodies fell under the authority of science and therefore should not be viewed and scrutinized by the general public.

By the 1940s, the freak show had lost almost all of its former prominence and popularity. Today, there are few freak shows left and many would argue that contemporary freak shows such as Ken Harck's Brothers Grim Sideshow, the 999 Eyes Freak Show, The Venice Beach Freak Show, and the various freak shows at Coney Island are curious nostalgia. Since the freak show has moved to the fringes of our society, "artists have attempted to assimilate its meanings to other media: words on the page, images on the screen. Beginning, that is to say, as a form of naïve or pop art, the freak show has become the subject matter of more self-conscious high art," and a more socially conscious and self-aware mass art (Fiedler 284). It is this transference of meaning that I will be exploring in much greater depth in the following chapters.

## Why We Look

At the heart of all freak shows is an indulgence in the human being's natural impulse to look at things that are interesting and unusual. We live in a highly visual world and, whether we are aware of it or not, what we see often dictates our beliefs, practices, and opinions. We look at the things and people in our lives in an effort to make sense of them and, therefore, the world: "To look is to actively make meaning of that world" (Sturken and Cartwright 10). Although it seems inherent and thus passive, looking *is* active, and to look at or away from something or someone is a choice. Because we choose whether or not to look, and because that choice can be influenced—we can make others look, be made to look, mutually exchange looks—it follows that looking "entails a play of power" (10). This power, of course, becomes more complicated when we examine who is looking, whom or what is being looked at, what the look communicates, and how the look is mediated.

As Rosemarie Garland-Thomson suggests, staring is a physiological response that has histories specific to different cultures. In other words, historical and cultural variables shape the meaning and practice of looking. Our natural urge to look at things that are novel or unexpected has been suppressed and guarded against over time with stories about the evil eye or simply the impulse of a mother telling her child, "don't stare!" We are not supposed to look at other people for prolonged periods of time because it makes them feel uncomfortable, it is rude, and it is often a way of non-verbally passing judgment. Hence, we are taught in the name of social propriety to suppress our natural desire to look. It makes sense then that freak shows were immensely popular in their time. Both the freak and the freak show institution grant permission to look through the exchange of money and by placing the freak in a performance-centered setting. By indulging the viewer's desire to look, the freak show eradicated a fissure between the things people wanted to look at and the things we have all been taught not to look at. Viewers paid for the rare opportunity to ignore the motherly voice in their heads reprimanding them from gawking at something or someone unusual, and instead were given permission to look at the things we have all been taught to look away from.

Since entering into a stare with someone involves an exchange of power, it only makes sense that we would prefer to stare on our own terms rather than being forced into staring by the unexpected presence of someone or something "starable" (Garland-Thomson 3–7). Hence, while we might be uncomfortable seeing a person with a physical disability on the street, we could enjoy looking at that same person in a permissible setting, such as on a stage or a screen. An excellent example of this comes from a very simple line from the movie *The Man Without a Face*, starring Mel Gibson as a man who was severely burned and deformed in a car accident. As a young boy sees him for the first time and gawks, his mother gives the famous line, "Don't stare" but follows it up with, "We are not at a circus." The implication is clear; we are not in a venue where it is permissible to stare at a freakish body. It is still a freakish body and we should still stare at it—but it is inappropriate in a space not structured around performance and in which the permission to stare has not been granted through the exchange of money or by the placement of the freak body onto a stage.

Though Garland-Thomson's *Staring* is an excellent and comprehensive study, additional scholarship on the subject suggests that, more than just a physiological impulse to stare, viewers are in fact simultaneously drawn to and repulsed by the freakish body for many different reasons. Critics disagree about whether the freak show was a space of disassociation or identification for its audiences, though most seem to argue the latter. Leslie Fiedler, among others, reassures us that the freak show was meant to be "therapeutic, cathartic, no matter what initial terror and insecurity it evokes. '*We* are the Freaks,' the human oddities are supposed to reassure us ... Not you. Not *you!*" (Fiedler 31). Hence, the disassociation the viewer feels when looking at a freak exhibit is a reassurance that the viewer is normal and nothing like the freaks onstage. Taking the opposite stance is Rachel Adams who suggests that while one would assume a detachment on the part of the viewer, as Fiedler does, it is in fact quite the opposite. In the act of staring at a freak, the viewer finds an opportunity to "project her own most hidden and perverse fantasies onto the freak and discovers them mirrored back in the freak's gaze" (Adams 8). In other words, staring at a freak may make us fear or even realize the freakishness within ourselves. So while there are varying ideas of what exactly propels people to want to look at unfamiliar or freakish bodies, it is clear that the freak show was successful because it gave people permission to indulge in their curiosities.

Nella Larsen's Harlem Renaissance novel *Quicksand* provides an excellent example of both identification and disassociation when Helga Crane, the novel's young mulatta protagonist, visits a freak show with her white friends in Copenhagen. When Helga and Axel Olsen, the famous artist who paints Helga's portrait and eventually proposes marriage to her, go to the vaudeville circus, they are witness to the display of two American racial freaks who sing and dance onstage to the great amusement of the audience. While her friends react with laughter and joy at the spectacle, Helga feels only shame and anger: "But she returned again and again to the Circus, always alone, gazing intently and solemnly at the gesticulating black figures, an ironical and silently speculative spectator" (Larsen 83). While the audience is clearly reassured by the separation between the men on stage and their own normality, and are therefore able to enjoy the show, Helga's identification seems to find her own freakishness mirrored back in the freak's gaze.

Helga is the only non-white member of her family and social circle in Copenhagen and thus is in the position to identify with the men at the freak show; she occupies the position of outsider within both her family and social units. When Helga becomes a "big hit" among the elite in Copenhagen, her family is immensely pleased; however, Helga feels as if she is "some new and strange species of pet dog being proudly exhibited." She thinks it is "[a]s if I had horns, or three legs," but she does not need to be physically disabled to wear the label of freak; her race freaks her well enough. In an all-white city, she is an oddity whose identity as freak is marked by her blackness: "Some stared [at Helga] surreptitiously, some openly, and some stopped dead in front of her in order more fully to profit by their stares" (73). Helga's friends and family, and the rest of the freak show's audience, however, are the norm, the majority, and so they could not possibly identify with the freaks on the stage.[3]

While individual experience seems to depend on the viewer's own freak/nonfreak status, as *Quicksand* clearly shows us, the mass response to the freak show is more telling of its cultural significance as an

---

[3] Parts of this discussion of *Quicksand* are excerpted from a previously published article of mine, "The Racial Freak: In and Out of Harlem" (*Storytelling: A Critical Journal of Popular Narrative*. vol. 12, no. 1 (Summer 2012): 5–14).

institution. The freak show served a cultural purpose beyond mere entertainment, and in many ways, the mass response to the freak show was
more significant than individual reactions because it reflected the serious
social and political issues of the time. As in my example from *Quicksand*,
Helga's identification, as well as her companions' disassociation with
the racial freaks on stage is representative of the power structures and
social anxieties in Helga's world. In making Helga a freak, her family is
asserting their power over her which is, in this case, an upper-class, white
power. Socially, their freaking of Helga is a way to come to terms with
their own racial prejudices and fears, and to become comfortable being
in the presence of such unfamiliar bodies. Whether they are laughing
at the racial freaks on stage, or praising the freakishness of Helga, the
power of looking at other bodies, in this case bodies which are anatomi-
cally different in an almost all-white Copenhagen, is astounding in that
it ascribes those bodies with meaning and context. To look at the freak
onstage is to demean and condemn, but to look at and celebrate Helga
as a freak is to work toward an understanding of difference.[4]

The spectacle of the racial freak has been popular since they were displayed in cartes de visite[5] as lynching victims and savages. James Allen's
*Without Sanctuary: Lynching Photography in America*, is one of many
collections that explores these photographs. Many of his images portray crowds of smiling, white spectators who had gathered to witness the
lynching as a form of communal entertainment. Thomas Fahy, whose
account of ethnographic freaks is as thorough as it is eye-opening, notes
that lynchings were often advertised ahead of time and people would
make occasions out of them, bringing their families, along with food
and drink, to celebrate the event. He describes the atmosphere of many
public lynchings as "carnival-like" and says that one could "mistake the
[image of the lynching] for a circus, convention, or concert" (21).

Fahy claims that such photographs might help the viewer to assuage
their fears about race and immigration because of the "safe context" they
provided for talking about non-white bodies; white viewers invited racial
bodies into their homes in innocuous ways and retained a safe distance

---

[4] One of the key differences between the two is, obviously, that the former is on a stage
and the latter a member of the social group who is freaking them.

[5] Small postcards of freaks. These were collector's items often distributed at freak shows.
See note 6.

from the black bodies in the photographs. On the other hand, however, he also acknowledges that images of freaks and lynching victims, which often "appear[ed] alongside each other in family albums," were enjoyed as souvenirs and celebrations and spoke to "white America's [in]ability to cope with racial difference... and contributed to racial tensions" (20).

The African American body was also displayed in freak shows, a form of exhibition which, like photography, maintained the distance between white viewers and black bodies. The black bodies on display at the freak show were alive, unlike those on display in lynching photographs, but they were made innocuous in other ways. Barnum's "What Is It?" exhibits, along with displays of "Lost Men" from remote places and even "Wild Men" from Africa, cast African Americans, sometimes with mental retardation or other disabilities, as stupid, childlike, and harmless. Racial spectacles were staged in other interesting ways as well. For example, Barnum arranged for an Arabian and an African American to face off in a boxing ring and highlighted their racial differences in his advertisements (Fahy 28–29).

Race was not the only social issue being explored by the freak show; concerns about gender and sexuality were also in the minds of many Americans. Leslie Fiedler argues that people are drawn to look at freakish bodies in large part because they remind us of our sexuality and that of others. He points to the changing body of the adolescent and the increasing awareness of the young adult's own sexuality as synonymous in many ways with what one would see at a freak show. During adolescence, there is a constant need to compare one's body with the bodies of others; it is from these comparisons that adolescents create their definitions of normalcy. Insecurities lead teenagers into feelings of being too much of one thing or not enough of another. In other words, pubescent girls may find themselves too big-breasted or too flat-chested, while boys might compare the size of their penises with others. Adolescents may also find their bodies to be too fat or too thin, and too hairy or not hairy enough. In addition to comparing themselves with members of the same sex, Fiedler notes that each sex tends to define their bodies as freakish in relation to the other; what a man has, the woman lacks, and vice versa. Because of our tendency to define our bodies in relation to the bodies of others, it makes sense that people would want to de-freak themselves by homogenizing their social groups and surrounding themselves with bodies that are similar to their own (31–32).

The freakish body, then, is a reminder of the traits we want to ignore. The fat lady and the human skeleton remind us, for example, that we too are either larger or smaller than others. The bearded woman reminds us of our own hair growth and the desire that comes with it to eliminate that hair with razors and waxes. Other sexual oddities such as hermaphrodites and men and women with malformed genitals call into question our belief in the bipolarity of the sexes. Ultimately, freakish bodies threaten illusions of black/white, male/female, and abled/disabled binaries and force the viewer to rethink common definitions of race, gender, and ability. In destabilizing these binaries, the freak/normal binary is also shaken because the former highlights that both terms are relative and therefore social constructions.

## How We Look

The illusion of intimacy and the reality of safe distance, as I will discuss throughout this book, have been essential in viewing the freak body throughout history. The gaze, defined as "not the act of looking itself, but the viewing relationship characteristic of a particular set of social circumstances" (Sturken and Cartwright 76), holds a normalizing power over people's bodies. Whether the photographic, cinematic, or televisual gaze, the body being looked at is being marked with normative meaning. Images of bodies most often tell viewers what bodies *should* look like, according to common perceptions of what is and isn't attractive, healthy, and normal. When viewers see images of these types of bodies, they digest the message that they too ought to look like those bodies. On the other hand, when presented with freakish bodies—bodies that tell viewers what they *should not* look like—the message is that these bodies are unhealthy, unnatural, unattractive, and undesirable. Often, the meaning inscribed upon freakish bodies is not quite this plain but is shrouded in ambiguity.

The changing frame of the freak show brings to mind Anne Friedberg's work on mobile viewing. In *The Virtual Window*, Friedberg says, "We know the world by what we see: through a window, in a frame, on a screen. As we spend more of our time staring into the frames of movies, television, computers, hand-held displays—'windows' full of moving images, text, icons, and 3-D graphics—how the world is framed may be as important as what is contained within that frame" (1). The freak show's frame has changed repeatedly since its inception, and each of these frames asks us to read the freak show in a different way. Despite the many different frames through which audiences have viewed the freak show, one facet has remained: its ability to keep emotional, temporal, and/or spatial distance between freak and viewer. The success of the freak show can be attributed in large part to its ability to keep this distance and to "simultaneously challenge and reinforce binaries" about bodies (Fahy 4).

However, as I have already noted, eventually (perhaps inevitably) the freak show stopped working as an outlet for confronting social, cultural, and political issues such as race, gender, and disability:

> As images of blackness, disability, and sexual ambiguity posed an increasing threat to white middle-class hierarchies and values, the desire to suppress and persecute visible difference intensified. The changes being brought on by modernity were making the boundaries between self and other—white/ black, male/female, able/disabled, heterosexual/homosexual—more and more tenuous, and the freak show was no longer a successful outlet for assuaging these social anxieties. Gradually, the crowds stopped coming. (Fahy 132)

The boundaries between freak and norm were collapsing in the wake of social and political progress. In other words, social progression suggested an equality that white, middle-class America was not prepared to accept. When he talks about the "distance" between viewer and object in the freak show, Fahy is talking about a perceived cultural difference, one indicative of power, normalcy, and superiority on the side of the viewer. Physically, viewer and object are rather close to one another, although human oddities "are never displayed at our level—the level of reality and the street outside." They were most often displayed on platforms above the audience so that viewers would need to look up to see them, or, as was often the case in the final "blow-off," they were displayed in pits in which case the viewer would need to look down to see them (see Fig. 2.1). (Fiedler 283). Though it is not a tremendous distance physically—freaks and their audiences are within mere feet of one another— the staging of the freak show creates a marked difference in the status of viewer and object.

Ironically, this staging unintentionally promoted exchanges between viewer and object. Freak shows were supposed to be places of restraint: "the customer is expected dutifully to absorb the spieler's monologue

**Fig. 2.1** A scene from Tod Browning's *Freaks* (Browning 1932) in which the crowd looks down into a freak show pit

while gazing at the prodigious body in awestruck wonder, then [make] a docile exit. However, historical evidence reveals how rarely this theory was realized in practice ... freaks talk back, the experts lose their authority, the audience refuses to take their seats" (Adams 13). It is logical that there should be such rowdy behavior at freak shows; after all, these shows invited conflict between different bodies. The viewer-object dynamic was not a sterile one; there was a tremendous amount of interaction as well as conflict between them.

The relationship between viewer and object, even over great physical and temporal distances, is never passive. Indeed, it is always an active two-way street. The creator of the image and the image itself do not produce meaning in and of themselves. In order to attain meaning, we must understand "how viewers interpret and experience the image" and "the context in which the image is seen" (Sturken and Cartwright 45). While producers of images certainly have an intended meaning in mind, they do not have full control over how their images are "read" by viewers. It is also significant to note that the gaze establishes relationships of power between viewer and object. The person looking generally has the power, and the object being stared at has little or no power. It follows that the image produced through the lens is a "central tool in establishing difference" (103). In systems of representation throughout history, binary oppositions such as those we have seen in the freak show are used to construct meaning about the other.

The freak show has always been about looking; that its rise in popularity coincided with the development of professional photography may be more than a lucky coincidence. The opportunity for audience members to bring a picture of a freak home with them was a tremendous selling point of early American freak shows. Between the 1860s and the early 1900s especially, freak portrait photographs were a wildly popular form of entertainment for Americans. As Robert Bogdan puts it, "The photo album was the television of Victorian homes" (11). Called cartes de visite, small portraits of freaks were popular freak show souvenirs.[6] In addition to displaying the freak's photo, these cards also provided biographies of their subjects on the back. Of course, these biographies were always exaggerated, if not completely fictional, accounts of the exhibit's life, written to make them appear more foreign and interesting to their audiences. Cartes de visite were immensely popular and allowed freak performers a certain level of celebrity; their images and names became common knowledge. There are countless examples, though one of the most famous is the portrait of Joseph Merrick (see Fig. 2.2), known as the Elephant Man, which displays Merrick in a formal Victorian three-piece suit, wearing a pocket-watch, with his hands in his lap. His portrait is only different from the many cartes de visite which passed hands every day because of his severely deformed face and right arm. Even today, a vast majority of people would recognize this specific image, even if they

---

[6]Cartes de visite do not refer only to portraits of freaks. Derived from the calling cards that were popular in the 1850s, cartes de visite became a sort of "social currency." These small formal portraits were most often of individuals or couples, or sometimes small families. The portraits were mounted on 2-1/2" × 4" sized cards and given to friends and family. This standard format was patented by Parisian photographer André Adolphe Disderi in 1854, who also developed a technique using a sliding plate holder and a camera with four lenses which allowed eight prints to be created with each negative (A Brief History of the Carte de Visite http://www.photographymuseum.com/histsw.htm).

**Fig. 2.2**   Joseph Merrick, "The Elephant Man" c. 1889

knew little or nothing about the Elephant Man. To be clear, freaks were certainly not considered a part of the middle- and upper-class Victorian community in whose dress and domestic settings they were often displayed, and by whom they were beloved; rather, the freak was "someone who reaffirmed the cultural superiority of the onlooker." As Bogdan notes, freaks were fascinating, welcome guests in Victorian homes, "as long as they stayed in their albums" (11).

Cinema gave spectators a new way to look at bodies. Christian Metz notes that "[c]inema is more perceptual … than many other means of expression"; this is why it has sometimes been referred to as "the synthesis of all the arts." Film "contains within itself the signifiers of other arts": it embodies music, pictures, sound, and photographs (731). It is interesting that such an encompassing form would succeed the live freak show because the decline of the freak show suggests a desire for disassociation with the freak body and yet, as film theorists have long argued, the cinematic image offers at least the promise of sensorial plentitude.

Though this plentitude is crucial for the medium, it has been understood, since at least Christian Metz, that we identity with a guiding person or protagonist first. Film theorists have argued that the spectator identifies primarily with the camera and secondarily with the protagonist. Mulvey, among others, has noted that in order to "suspend one's disbelief" and immerse oneself in the narrative of a film, "one must first 'identify with' the camera itself as if it were one's own eyes and thus accept the viewpoint offered" (Chandler). The intimate connection to the image, rather than the spectacle, is then what characterizes film spectatorship. In narrative cinema, the art of looking has been understood in relation to voyeurism. Chandler explains that "a key feature of the gaze is that the object of the gaze is not aware of the current viewer (though they may originally have been aware of being filmed, photographed, painted etc. and may sometimes have been aware that strangers could subsequently gaze at their image)" (Chandler). Voyeurism is implicit in viewing and this, of course, implies a relationship of power, "in which the gazer is superior to the object of the gaze" (Chandler qt. Schroader).

Additional to this power play is the fact that the cinematic image is understood as both absent and present. Many of the ideas considered foundational in apparatus and spectatorship theories are indebted to post-structuralism, namely the theories of Louis Althusser. Jean-Louis Baudry, Raymond Bellour, and Christian Metz, along with Jacques Lacan, Roland Barthes, and Michel Foucault, all "argued in different ways that the self-awareness of human subjectivity is founded on a central misrecognition by the subject—or self, or ego—that it is somehow central to the processes of knowing the world." Essentially, they all argue that "the subject's knowledge of world and self is shaped by discourse … which produces and reproduces [their own] subjectivity and, often enough, its constitutive illusions" (Rosen 156–157). The viewer both shapes and is shaped by their position as spectator. This interpellation is significant especially when exploring cultural messages that are sent through media such as film because culturally constructed concepts of beauty, race, gender, and sexuality, for example, are made to seem inherent when they are in fact socially constructed.

While many post-structural film theorists simply invoke Lacan's theory of the "mirror stage," in which an infant sees itself in the mirror and recognizes itself as "other" for the first time, Christian Metz complicates and extends this notion by arguing that the film screen is not a mirror because the spectator does not see himself on the screen and cannot really identity with other objects as the self. Therefore, the only thing he identifies with on the screen is the other:

> At the cinema, it is always the other who is on the screen; as for me, I am there to look at him. I take no part in the perceived, on the contrary, I am *all-perceiving*. All-perceiving as one says all-powerful ...; All-perceiving, too, because I am entirely on the side of the perceiving instance: absent from the screen, but certainly present in the auditorium, a great eye and ear without which the perceived would have no one to perceive it, the instance, in other words, which *constitutes* the cinema signifier (it is I who make the film)...In the cinema, the subject's knowledge takes a very precise form without which no film would be possible. This knowledge is dual (but unique). I know I am perceiving something imaginary ... and I know it is I who am perceiving it". (734)

The spectator is aware of the fourth wall, the audience around them, the screen, the projector, and the fact that they, the spectator, is the one observing all of it. Thus, the viewing experience is not limited to identification with one's own ego, or the other, but is potentially much more dispersed.

Furthering the idea of a compound spectator experience, Linda Williams has argued for multiple viewing positions afforded to the spectator by narrative cinema. In her revision of Laura Mulvey and the major strain of feminism and psychoanalysis in film, she argues that the spectator no longer only occupies a single position in relation to the bodies on screen but can occupy dual and even contradictory positions. She contends, through a close reading of *Stella Dallas*, that "double vision," or the idea that female spectatorship is multiply identified, is a common experience for the female viewer. She explains:

> Unlike the male who must constantly differentiate himself from his original object of identification [the mother] in order to take on a male identity, the woman's ability to identify with a variety of different subject positions [because she does not need to differentiate from the mother to form her identity] makes her a very different kind of spectator ... [one who is] in a constant state of juggling all positions at once". ("Something Else..." 19)

The viewer's compound positionality allows us to see that when viewing the freak body, the film spectator, much like the audience member at a freak show, can simultaneously feel horror, fear, and disgust, while still relating to the freak body.

In *Freaks*, which I will further unpack in my next chapter, the viewer initially identifies with Cleopatra who is a norm among freaks. However, when she is revealed as a potential murderer, our identification shifts to that of the freaks—Hans and Frieda, in particular. Finally, the viewer is forced to turn their identification inward when the freak body and the normal body collide in the film's final scenes: are we "one of [them]" or are we normal? The film's notions of good, evil, freakishness, and normality are ambivalent and thus, as a viewer, our identification is split and even at times contradictory.

Though it has similarities to film, television is unique in its availability, intimacy, and possession of other media (television supersedes film as a "synthesis of all the arts": we can watch film, documentary, internet clips, and music videos all on television). Bourdieu believes that television, "by virtue of its reach and exceptional power, ... produces effects which, though not without precedent, are completely original" (Bourdieu 238). Auslander also acknowledges this, saying that "[t]elevision [can be] characterized as a hybrid of existing forms. [It is] radio with sight, movies with a zest of immediacy, theatre (intimate or spectacular) with all seats about six rows back and in the centre [sic], tabloid opera and circus without peanut vendors" (15). Whereas film lies in the "realm of memory, repetition, and displacement in time," television "occurs only in the now" (15). The immediacy of television is significant in that the viewer, through the illusion of close proximity to the event being witnessed, produces the feeling of television's intimacy; thus the home becomes a kind of "theatre (sic) characterized, paradoxically, by both absolute intimacy and global reach" (16).

Some have argued that due to its casual nature, the viewer has a different relationship to looking at television, stating that television demands a mere "glance," rather than a "gaze" and that, therefore, "the 'voyeuristic mode' cannot be as intense for the television viewer as for the cinema spectator" (Chandler qt. Ellis). However, as I suggest in Chap. 4, voyeurism is implicit in reality television and therefore the viewer's sense of intimacy and association is amplified, not lessened. The television viewer feels closer to the freak body because that body is inserted into the viewer's living room, but also because the viewer is allowed access into the freak's "real" intimate space as well. The reciprocal nature of this relationship suggests that the television viewer is both aware of himself as a producer of the gaze, but can also identify with the object of the gaze. Indeed, the lure of reality television stardom is that it casts "ordinary people" doing extraordinary things or in bizarre circumstances, or extraordinary people doing mundane, everyday things. In either case, the viewer feels a sense of identification with the person who is either living a covetous life or who mirrors the viewer's own life.

While it is important to individually understand the ways audiences look at and understand the freak body through the frames of photography, film, and television, today's technology is moving forward at such a rapid pace that the "differences between the media of movies, television, and computers are rapidly diminishing" as new technologies emerge (Friedberg 439). Each successive media has been usurped by its predecessor and while each screen "retain[s] their separate location ... the types of images you see on each of them are losing their medium-based specificity" (439). Audiences can access photographs, movies, videos, music, television shows, and porn—as I will discuss in Chap. 5—literally in the palms of our hands. Smartphones, laptops, and tablets have made entertainment as close, intimate, and safe as ever, and yet these new technologies have also brought down the screens separating us from the formerly untouchable other.

## CHAPTER 3

# Horror Movies, Horror Bodies: Blurring the Freak Body in Cinema

This chapter examines the freak body as a sight of spectacle and con-flict in film, specifically in the genres of horror and melodrama. The por-trayal of such bodies has been problematic in film, especially in horror. While this is not particularly surprising, given Hollywood's marginali-zation and misrepresentation of women and minority racial and ethnic groups, it is an area of concern that has not been as fully explored as the representation of different types of otherness in cinema. Recent work in disability studies has, in general, focused on filmic representations of dis-ability in documentaries and dramas rather than horror and fantasy films. According to David Church, this is because the realistic world of the film closely resembles, if not directly represents, the world in which real peo-ple with real disabilities exist, and if people study problems of representa-tion in order to correct them or to help develop progressive viewpoints, then it is logical to study the representation that most closely resembles the world in which progress can happen. While the realistic depiction of disability in film is certainly a significant area of exploration, it seems to me that the disabled body has been more visible in horror than in any other film genre, and is thus in need of more critical attention than it has to date received.

The examination of the freak body in film is significant within my overall argument because of the freak body's movement from the freak show to the film screen. This movement, both temporal and spa-tial, marks a change in the viewer-object relationship and consequently between freak and norm. The separation of time and space that is created

© The Author(s) 2017
J.L. Williams, *Media, Performative Identity, and the New American Freak Show*, DOI 10.1007/978-3-319-66462-0_3

between viewer and freak in the movie theater is replaced with physical closeness between viewer and freak on screen. In horror, it is the collision of different bodies which blurs the lines between freakish and normal and thus elicits fear in the audience.

Like the freak show, horror has traditionally been seen by most as a lowbrow form of entertainment, one of the reasons why disability studies has not given the genre much critical attention. Church notes that "[b]oth freak shows and fantastic films appear to frame the disabled body in an exploitative performance space (i.e. the stage/screen) somewhere at the boundaries of a normative society, presided over by a mediating non-disabled agent (i.e. the showman/filmmaker) for the amusement, shock, and wonder of a voyeuristic audience" (Church).[1] Given these similarities, it was only a matter of time, really, before the freak show itself appeared on the film screen. However, as I will argue, the horror film allows for a different, more reflective relationship between freak and norm than the freak show.

Tod Browning's *Freaks*, a horror film about the lives of freak show and circus performers, was the central catalyst in cinema's appropriation of the freak body in horror. My exploration of the film lays the groundwork for my later discussion of human monsters in *Psycho* and *Rosemary's Baby*. I use these horror classics as stepping stones to *The Texas Chainsaw Massacre* and the lesser-known film *The Funhouse*, which confront forms of otherness in notable ways. Ultimately, my readings of these films illustrate how the horror in horror movies happens when normal bodies come into direct contact with freak bodies. Thus, even though film moves the freak body away from the viewer in space and time, it moves the normal body much closer to the freak body—they are often in direct contact—on screen.

Because film spectatorship allows multiple identifications for the viewer, horror opens up the possibility of both demonizing and identifying with the freak. To draw out the persistence of identification, I will end the chapter by focusing on melodramas about disability—films that discuss disability in the "real world" and often feature a disabled protagonist.[2] My discussion is anchored in *The Elephant Man*'s representation

---

[1] Here, Church uses the term "fantastic films" to combine the genres of horror and fantasy.

[2] It is worth noting that these disabled characters are nearly always played by non-disabled actors, except in cases when it is unavoidable such as when the character is a little

of disability which plays on the paradigm of the disabled person as an object of pity, or as a moral compass whose purpose is to teach the non-disabled something about the value of life. Ultimately, these explorations will serve as support for my argument that horror's viewer-object relationship makes its treatment of freaks more complex than we see on the surface by blurring the lines between normal and freakish bodies.

## What We Fear in Freaks

*Freaks* has been written about in most freak and circus scholarship since the 1970s, so its place here is requisite.[3] It has become such a point of concern in literature about freaks and freak shows for two central reasons: the first is that it was groundbreaking in its style (it is a horror film that, at times, mimics documentary), content, and casting choices; and the second is that MGM pulled *Freaks* from theaters after a brief run of only a few months, and it was banned from audiences in the UK for thirty years after its 1932 release. While others have focused on the ostensible fact of disabled bodies, my discussion primarily focuses on the freak-norm relationship and the ambiguous representations of disability in *Freaks*. My ultimate concern lies in the ways that freakish bodies are mediated by cinema, a concern that hinges on the very relationships between normal and freakish bodies within the film.

Since its resurrection as a cult favorite in the 1960s, *Freaks* has become a sort of landmark text in the modern study of sideshow. In fact, it has become, as Rachel Adams states, "the foundational text through which authors and artists in the twentieth century came to understand the freak show" (63). While Adams may be overstating the point, she is correct in implying that the film has had a dramatic impact on freak show scholarship. This is problematic because, despite that it often feels like a documentary, *Freaks* is a fictional story about freakish bodies; yet, this fact has not stopped it from becoming "a point of reference for all subsequent representations of [freak show] culture" (63).

---

person (although there is the notable exception of the 2003 romantic comedy *Tiptoes* in which Gary Oldman plays a dwarf).

[3] Examples include Rachel Adams' *Sideshow U.S.A.*, Robert Bogdan's *Freak Show*, Thomas Fahy's *Freaks Shows and the Modern American Imagination*, and Leslie Fiedler's *Freaks*.

*Freaks* has done more than develop a filmic link to the freak show, as Adams argues. It has, in fact, transposed the freak show from the carnival to the screen, and thus the reason *Freaks* is a "foundational text" is because it has acted as a catalyst for the medium of film to appropriate the cultural function of the freak show while simultaneously undoing the freak show's distancing of viewer and object. Where Adams is shortsighted here is in the fact that she only recognizes *Freaks* as having replaced the actual freak show in terms of an object of study to inform critics and theorists about an entity which no longer exists. In other words, because the freak show can no longer be a primary source of information, critics have used *Freaks* as the next best thing. The usage of *Freaks* as a historical source is an inappropriate replacement because *Freaks*, by its very nature as a film, cannot directly duplicate the live freak show (a point I will return to later because it is such a crucial idea). However, very little attention has been paid to the differences that come along with the appropriation of the live freak show to scripted and recorded film. In taking a live show and replacing it with a filmed facsimile, *Freaks* has become just as foundational within the medium of cinema as it has in freak show discourse. It has informed and perhaps even directed the representation of freak bodies, not just in "freak cinema," as Adams suggests, but in other genres—horror, fantasy, drama—as well.

Loosely adapted from Tod Robbins' short story, "Spurs," *Freaks* presents a dual narrative that is part pseudo-documentary and part narrative. In other words, the beginning of the film feels like a documentary in that it takes us inside the world of a traveling carnival and provides audiences with a new level of access. The beginning of the film is comprised of short vignettes of the various carnival and sideshow performers. Browning famously cast real freak show performers including, among others, the famous Siamese twins, Daisy and Violet Hilton; Johnny Eck, the half-boy; Prince Randian, the human torso; and Josephine-Joseph, the half-man/half-woman. More significant to the plot is the dwarf couple Hans and Frieda, played by siblings Harry and Daisy Earles, around whom the narrative tension centers.[4] Two norm couples fill out the cast:

---

[4] Known as the Doll Family, the siblings, Harry and Daisy Earles, were probably the most successful of all the performers in *Freaks*. Along with their sisters Gracie and Tiny, the Doll Family traveled the USA and Europe performing in various circuses, sideshows, and vaudeville acts from the 1920s until the 50s when they retired their act (Fiedler 63–64). Of the siblings, Harry had the most successful film career, and it was Harry, in fact, who urged MGM to buy the right to "Spurs" in the first place (Larsen and Haller 166).

Cleopatra, the Amazonian trapeze artist and her lover Hercules, the ultra-masculine strongman; and Venus and Phroso, a circus performer and a clown.

The vignettes that make up the film's first half have the feel of a documentary primarily because the cast upon whom they are focused are not actors, but rather real people playing versions of themselves. Mirroring the episodic feel of the freak show stage, and thus the performers' real-life acts, these cut-scenes showcase the abilities and talents of the freak performers. For example, Prince Randian, the human torso—called such because he has neither arms nor legs—is featured lighting his own cigarette, an impressive part of his real-life act. Other freaks are shown doing everyday tasks that are fascinating because of the individual's disabilities, such as when we see Frances O'Conner, the armless girl, feed herself using her foot, or Johnny Eck, who has no legs, using his arms to move his body with agility and deftness.[5]

The other half of the film, in which a narrative plot is finally developed, follows Earles' character, Hans, as he falls in love with Cleopatra, much to the dismay of his fiancée, Frieda. Cleopatra, whom Hans calls "the most beautiful big woman" he has ever seen, patronizes and mocks Hans until she finds out that he has a rather large fortune. Pretending to return his admiration, she tricks him into marriage and then she and her lover Hercules plot to kill him, allowing them to run away with Hans' money. Typically, Hans is viewed by critics as foolish and weak, falling prey to the desire to be with a "normal" woman.

The film's centerpiece scene is the couple's wedding feast, a scene as fascinating as it is disturbing and uncomfortable. The camera focuses on a large banquet table around which the freaks are sitting; Cleopatra and Hercules stand out as the sole norms. A drunken Hans is treated like a naughty child by his cruel and impatient new wife, while the freaks try to welcome Cleopatra to their brethren with a chant of, "Gooble, Gobble,

---

[5] These are striking examples of the supercrip paradigm, a trope that sees people with disabilities as inspirational for doing everyday tasks that were it not for the individual's functional limitations, would not be seen as extraordinary. While this may seem at first like a positive image of disability, it is just as harmful as paradigms that see people with disabilities as needing fixing or objects of pity. Many disability scholars feel that such stereotyping "remain[s] the most significant obstacle to normal interaction between nondisabled and disabled people" (Shapiro 16–18). I offer a lengthier discussion of this concept towards the end of this chapter.

one of us!" Horrified at the thought of being considered comparable to sideshow freaks, Cleopatra scolds Hans and assaults the table with screams of "Freaks! Freaks!" until they scatter. We soon find out that Cleopatra is slowly poisoning Hans, making him appear ill to the others. When Hans and the other freaks discover the truth about Cleopatra, they plot against both her and Hercules.

The film's penultimate scene is arguably the scariest of the entire film. As the circus travels through the rainy night, the freaks stop the caravan, overturn Cleopatra's trailer, and attack her. The violence, though only suggested, is heightened because "their prey are lit only by occasional flashes of lightening, and the camera remains fixed at [the freaks'] level so that we can see what happens only intermittently and through their eyes" (Fiedler 294). The film implies that the freaks attack both Cleopatra and Hercules, though we only see them advancing and do not see the attack itself. *Freaks* ends with an image of Cleopatra as a mutilated chicken woman in a sideshow exhibit—a scarred, beaked face; her body covered in feathers; no legs; webbed hands; and only the ability to squawk, not speak[6]—bringing back to our minds images of the freaks chanting "One of us! One of us!" Generally, Cleopatra's transformation into a freak through a violent punishment has been read negatively because it makes us consider the origins of the real freaks' disabilities throughout the film, the suggestion being that the freak body is a life-sentence for moral depravity or violence.

A large part of *Freaks'* negative public reception was that it was released during a time when the viewer's relationship to the freak show was changing. As I have detailed in Chap. 2, people had stopped going to freak shows almost entirely by the 1930s because of a cultural shift in attitudes toward the freak body. Science had become more progressive in preventing and treating physical disability, and the medical model of

---

[6] Before its initial release, *Freaks* was heavily edited by Irving Thalberg, MGM's production supervisor. In the unedited version, Hercules and Phroso fight until a wagon falls and crushes Hercules' legs; Hercules almost escapes but before he does the freaks close in on him. As for Cleopatra, "lightening topples a great tree and Cleopatra is caught under it!" The freaks swarm and attack and, though we do not see them maim her, we hear murderous screams. The drivers of the caravan soon discover her mutilated body and "cry for a doctor" (*Freaks*: Script Synopsis). Most fascinating, is that "the deleted shots showed a passing implication that [Hercules] was deprived of his manhood ... With the story's return to the dime museum, Hercules is found singing in a tenor falsetto, perhaps some love song to his mutilated Cleo" (Savada).

disability, which saw people with disabilities as needing healing or fixing, was growing more popular. This paradigm shift resulted in a decline in the popularity of the freak show.

*Freaks* failed, in part, because it confronted people with the presence of freakish bodies, but this is not the only element that stopped people from embracing the film. I contend that audiences were turned off by two key elements. The first is that *Freaks* shattered illusions about people with disabilities in showing them doing things that non-disabled audiences also did—eating, socializing, giving birth—a spectacle not unlike what would have been seen, or at least suggested, at the freak show. Especially unsettling for viewers is the suggestion of sexuality and gender ambiguity in the film. Robin Larsen & Beth Haller's "The Case of *Freaks*" provides an excellent overview of the public reception and rejection of *Freaks*, and what this rejection means about our society's relationship to differently-abled bodies. Their discussion of disability and sexuality is especially interesting.[7] The article stresses the physical differences between the sexually involved characters, Hans and Cleopatra in particular: "Hans stresses his 'abnormal' sexual desire" when he tells Cleopatra that "most big people [laugh at him because] they don't realize that [he is] a man with the same feelings they have" (166). Perhaps subtle by today's standards, such a line would have been seen as quite suggestive in the 1930s. After all, the implication is that Hans is not too small to have intercourse with Cleopatra, an innuendo that leaves viewers wondering about the logistics of such a contrasting physical match. Many of the film's other sexual suggestions leave viewers wondering things like "How do Siamese twins make love?" (166–167) and "What is under Joseph/Josephine's costume?" Larsen and Haller feel that such suggestions made audiences "uncomfortable rather than titillating them" (170). However, I would argue that it made them uncomfortable specifically *because* it titillated them. It is clear that audiences were made uncomfortable by the suggestion of abnormal bodies as sexual bodies. The film covers over this discomfort with the "appropriate" sexual

---

[7]Although an excellent article, Larsen and Haller somehow make the error of referring to Cleopatra as Venus throughout almost the entirety of the piece. While such a tremendous oversight calls into question the overall academic value of the essay, I feel that it is quite a good piece—and a valuable one—in every other regard. I will be altering direct quotes from the article to correct this error.

pairings we end up with at the end of *Freaks*, namely Hans and Frieda—both freaks—and Phroso and Venus—both norms.

The second and more significant reason for *Freaks'* failure, in terms of this study, is that *Freaks* collapsed the distance between norm and freak that had been established by the actual freak show. While it was always careful to stress the differences between viewer and object, *Freaks* directly confronts the relationship between the two. Such confrontation unsettled the average viewer who was able, possibly for the first time, to experience self-reflection as part of the "freak show." Unfortunately for MGM and *Freaks*, such self-reflection quickly led to fear and insecurity because it allowed the viewer to see themselves reflected in the anchoring "normal" protagonists, as well as in the film's freaks, and thus realize that they could become disabled themselves, not just blurring the line between viewer and object, but crossing it completely.

The audience is ambivalent about which characters they are supposed to identify with on the screen. Hans, a logical choice because he is victimized by Cleopatra, is never really a sympathetic character because of the way he treats Frieda (who may be the most truly innocent, sympathetic, and normal character in the film). Viewers cannot sympathize with a man who treats the woman who loves him so poorly. The starring characters in *Freaks* are humanized in the fact that not one of them is all good or all bad—even Frieda has some negative characteristics; she is a pushover who's willing to take abuse from Hans. Further complicating issues of viewer identification is that the narrative perspective continually shifts throughout the film. The viewer is instructed by these narrative shifts to occupy a space of dual identification. Audiences are initially drawn to the normal bodies on screen, but quickly transfer our identification to the freaks when they are victimized by Cleopatra. By providing the audience few normal bodies with which to identify, the film assumes the audience's identification with and then rejection of Cleopatra. She is, like the audience, a norm in a world of freaks. Thus, Cleopatra becomes a stand-in for the audience in mirroring their fears within the film. She is horrified when the freaks tell her she is one of them, and of course she does become a disabled freak at the end of the film.

If Cleopatra is a stand-in for the able-bodied viewer, then her closeness with the freaks is frightening and her fate is all too real a possibility. As Tobin Siebers explains:

Only 15 percent of people with disabilities are born with their impairments. Most people become disabled over the course of their life. This truth has been accepted only with difficulty by mainstream society; it prefers to think of people with disabilities as a small population, a stable population ... Most people do not want to consider that life's passage will lead them from ability to disability. The prospect is too frightening, the disabled body, too disturbing. (*Disability Theory* 59)

To be disabled means to enter unwillingly into a new subject position, one wrought with physical and social challenges that will, at least in part, redefine a person's identity. Thus Cleopatra is doomed to experience some of society's greatest fears: the fear of losing control, of losing the body, of becoming unattractive, and of becoming an outcast. The disabling of an able-bodied person in *Freaks* makes disability palpable and brings it closer to home for the viewer.

*Freaks*, and audience reactions to it, reinforced the cultural link between morality and disability. This paradigm takes the form of two extremes: the disabled person is thought of as either morally superior or morally corrupt. *Freaks*, with its violent ending—turning a norm woman into a freak—reinforces the latter, the cultural assumption that a bad outside is equivalent to a bad inside. We have historically been presented with the idea that freakish bodies only belong to those who are violent, degenerate, or stupid. Examples abound in figures such as Captain Hook, Richard III, fairytale witches, and countless comic book villains such as Two-Face and the Joker. In *Freaks* this is portrayed by the freaks' attack on the norms—they choose to enact revenge in a violent and evil way and, as a result, audiences would assume that they are morally corrupt. But this concept is especially reinforced by Cleopatra's freakification: it is difficult not to feel like she deserves everything she gets at the film's end. Hence, the freaks only bring her inner ugliness to the surface. She is made a freak because she is so immoral.

Critical and viewer responses to the film were also morally complex. For example, "The Case of Freaks" cites an excerpt from a letter written by the head of the Motion Picture Producers and Distributors Association, Frances Diehl, who identifies the freaks cast in the film as victims in need of defending. He says:

At a time when every effort is being made to raise audience standards, a company is attempting to foist on the public the lowest form of amusement – a circus side show where one may peep at the deformities and abnormalities of human beings. It is a cruel and revolting thing and we

> raise our protest ... It is incomprehensible that [MGM] ... will stoop
> to the disgrace of making dollars out of hurt, disfigured, and suffering
> humanity. (Larsen and Haller qt. Diehl 168)

Such a complaint wrongfully assumes the suffering of people with disabilities. In an effort to protect the disabled, such critics are actually doing them a disservice. An excellent example is given in the opening of *Sideshow U.S.A.*, in which Adams recounts the story of Otis Jordan, the Frog Man, a side show freak who was angered and insulted when a concerned citizen protested his exhibition as a freak, citing it to be inhumane and degrading. Jordan's response has been that of many freaks in the same position: he enjoyed his work as a freak and was offended that someone would speak for him and assume to know what was in his best interests (1). Such good-natured attempts to help or save "exploited" side show acts have historically ignored the wants of the acts themselves, and have resulted in many performers being unemployed—a position far more degrading than making a good living for oneself on one's own terms. In the case of *Freaks*, not only was the cast not "hurt" and "suffering," many cite the filming of *Freaks* to be among their happiest memories (Savada).

The ultimate horror in *Freaks* is not simply in putting freak bodies on screen. That the film was rejected, panned by both audiences and critics, suggests something more than manufactured horror: it presents real-life possibilities (a freak marrying a norm, for instance) that were simply too real for audiences. Thus the film enters into the horror genre through the blurring between normal and freakish bodies. *Freaks* is a frame story; it begins and ends with a sideshow barker talking up the "living, breathing monstrosities" in his freak show. Not sixty seconds into the film, the barker tells the audience that "but for the accidents of birth, you might be even as they are. They did not ask to be brought into the world, but into the world they came." The barker quickly ushers the crowd over to a lowered pit exhibit into which film audiences cannot see (see Fig. 2.1). The reactions of the film's crowd as they peer down into the exhibit—a woman screaming, people turning their heads away, expressions of disgust—tell the viewer that the freak exhibit is indeed a horrible sight. The barker then tells the crowd the story of how Cleopatra was once a beautiful trapeze artist who was considered "the peacock of the air." This story is, of course, the film's central storyline which I have already discussed. At the film's close, the viewer returns to this frame and here the barker finally allows us to look upon Cleopatra, now as a deformed chicken woman.

This frame serves various purposes. Although the film enters the world of the freak, the frame shrouds the film in normality and assures the viewer that they are entering the freak show through the normative gaze. As if we, too, were at a freak show, our interest is piqued by the opening frame and by the end of *Freaks* we cannot wait to see what is waiting for us in the exhibit. Viewers are left with a shocking image that simultaneously makes the film horrifying and ridiculous. We are frightened when we see what has become of Cleopatra, and her freakification is the film's final and most assertive way of telling the viewer that disability is something that can happen to anyone at any time, particularly if that person has acted in immoral ways. In exploiting Hans and therefore the freak body, Cleopatra sentences herself to a fate in which her body becomes a freakish spectacle. With her freakification, *Freaks* holds a mirror up to its viewers and forces them to question their own relationship to the freak body. In a sense, her freakification becomes our own. However, at the same time, her nearly cartoonish embodied form at the end keeps the fear of our own freakification at a distance. While we can all become disabled, becoming a chicken/human hybrid is obviously not a realistic depiction of disability. *Freaks* threatens us with the loss of our own normal bodies while at the same time reassures us that we are not living in the same reality of the film. In other words, the nature of Cleopatra's freak body says to us, "Don't worry—it's only a movie."[8] This metacinematic moment creates a dual narrative focus that will be picked up on in subsequent horror, as my next section discusses.

## Why Horror?

*Freaks* was never a mainstream success, even after its rerelease, and its cult status, while significant in its own right, makes it a poor example to gage society's preoccupations at the time of its renewal. To be clear, its

---

[8] The reprieve from the world of the freak is a plot device that I have noticed in many other texts. Examples include the telekinetic abilities of Chick in *Geek Love*, the mummified Egyptian who comes to life in Annette Curtis Klausse's *Freaks*, the ridiculous psychological explanation given at the end of *Psycho*, and of course the freaking of Cleopatra in *Freaks*. These instances are the only unrealistic or otherworldly devices in otherwise realistic narratives. They are used, I believe, to offer a reassurance that the freak body is a distant reality.

rejection when it was first released certainly *does* speak to society's cultural attitudes at the time, as it was released by a major studio who envisioned the film as a commercial Hollywood horror movie that could rival the recent successes of Universal's "new horror cycle" (Larsen and Haller 165). In other words, *Freaks* was envisioned and promoted as a mainstream film, and it was the average American audience who rejected it. It was not, however, the average American audience who embraced it upon its rerelease in 1962, but rather film aficionados and horror enthusiasts.

Thus, a better point of examination for my purposes is the rise of horror films that, working in the tradition of *Freaks*, brought the freak body back to the big screen, questioned what it means to be a freak, and commented on the freak-norm relationship. Unlike *Freaks*, however, these films do this in a way that suggests the viewer is unwilling or unable to view the freakish body in an overt way. The disabled body is not a central focus *as* a disabled body in most horror the way that it is in *Freaks*. In other words, the disabled or freaked body is used as a tool to evoke fear or pity, but is rarely discussed and is not treated as a disability. As Robert Bogdan notes, "In horror films the association of evil with disability is ... ubiquitous. Horror film 'monsters' are scarred, deformed, disproportionally built, hunched over, exceptionally large, exceptionally small, deaf, speech impaired, visually impaired, mentally ill, or mentally subnormal" (vii). The freak body tends, in most horror films, to appear as either victim or monster and is not always physically disabled in clearly recognizable ways, but is more often mutilated, deformed, and/or sexually dysfunctional.

Through horror, cinema is able to be more disclosing because of the contact it allows us with the freak body, but also more removed than the freak show in its examinations of the freak body. The camera allows us to see the freak body in seemingly unrestricted ways. Of course the viewer is seeing what the camera chooses to show and is thus not *really* unrestricted, although it certainly feels that way at times. Audiences are privy to the intimate moments of the freak body in ways not permitted by the freak show; my later discussions, especially of *The Elephant Man* and *The Funhouse*, will illustrate this. On the other hand, the camera is positioned as the normal gaze, thus we are never viewing the freak body through the eyes of the freak. Viewers only gain access to the freak body because we are doing so through a normative lens. In the fleeting moments that we do take the position of freak, our perception is altered in marked ways—a late scene in *The Elephant Man* in which we look through Merrick's eyes underscores this. The only scene in which the viewer occupies the freak's gaze—the theater scene—is one of marked visual deformation from the rest of the film. Images become distorted, time and space seem to shift, and it is difficult to comprehend exactly what Merrick sees when he looks at the stage. This highlights the fact that audiences cannot occupy the gaze of the freak but can only gaze *at* the freak from a normative perspective.

Horror is, more than any other film genre, formulaic and redundant. Audiences tend to know exactly what is going to happen, who the next victim will be, and sometimes even how they will die. Carol Clover, in her exploration of gender in modern horror films, points out that the horror film's "total predictability did not create boredom or disappointment. On the contrary, the predictability was clearly the main source of pleasure, and the only occasion for disappointment would have been a modulation of the formula, not the repetition of it" (Clover qt. Britton 9). More than finding comfort in familiarity, the positive response to such redundancy speaks to the normalizing effect of such repetition. In other words, if the pattern keeps working it must be because it is "right," and if the viewer can relate to it then they must be "alright."

Horror writer Stephen King believes that audiences crave horror movies because they allow us to "dare our nightmares" and to prove "that we can [face our fears], that we are not afraid." He also cites our need to be reassured of our own normalcy, which is one of the key crowd-drawing factors of the freak show. While he does not make the freak show connection, he does say that "Freda Jackson as the horrible melting woman in *Die, Monster, Die!* confirms for us that no matter how far we may be removed from the beauty of a Robert Redford or a Diana Ross, we are still light-years from true ugliness" (King). In other words, the viewer may not feel normal or attractive but is reassured by the fact that they are more normal and more attractive than horror's freaks. But audiences also go to horror films because they are fun. As King notes, horror films "urge us to put away our more civilized and adult penchants for analysis and to become children again, seeing things in pure black and whites." His phrasing is interesting because, while his point is that horror is simple and easy to read, so much of what we see in horror is *not* black and white. Further, horror's ambiguity often evokes the fearful and uncomfortable reactions of its viewers.

This in-betweenness or blurring, including between able- and disabled bodies, is a staple of the horror film. The maiming and disfiguring of bodies that is so emblematic of the genre is a way for horror to work through problematic representations of disabled bodies. The scariness of horror often comes from the closeness and interaction between "normal" and different bodies and, more than any other genre, horror seizes the opportunity presented by cinema to collapse the separation that so often exists between such bodies. Thus, the horror film serves a similar purpose to the freak show while claiming its own identity. This closeness to the freak body affords the viewer the voyeuristic pleasure of looking without fear of retribution. The darkened theater is a safe space to confront otherness while disguising the look at the body as a look at the fantastic. In other words, viewers are given permission to stare at forbidden bodies—freakish bodies—because they are presented to them as fictional monsters. Christian Metz suggests that disavowal—when one denies a more perceptional belief in favor of a more primal one—is inscribed into film. So, the viewer can *know* that they fear the freakish body and yet *believe* that they are just watching fiction, or the viewer can *know* that they are watching a fiction and yet *believe* that the freakish body is a bad and scary body.

To see a horror movie is to experience a thrill that, while difficult perhaps to describe, speaks to cultural memories. Kendall R. Phillips anecdotally recounts the hundreds of stories people have told him about their horror movie memories. The storytellers can connect seeing a particular horror film with a specific time, place, and reaction, and each had strong memories of the thrill of true fear that existed both during and after watching the film, and how this thrill kept them going back for more. Phillips notes that "[h]orror films, perhaps more than any other type of film, seem to impact people's lives," although he does point out that the majority of these experiences occur while adolescents "are beginning to struggle with societal boundaries and forbidden knowledge" (1–2). Phillips brings me back to my first memorable horror experience: watching *Candyman* (1992) as an eleven year old. While I can no longer recall the movie's plot, I have a vivid memory of my reaction to the movie's legend, which was that if you repeated "Candyman" into your mirror five times, he would appear and kill you with his hooked hand. Every night for months, I draped a thick blanket over my bedroom mirror before going to sleep. Such a strong reaction is indicative of the trauma horror films can afflict on their viewers. Because you must be an active participant in summoning the Candyman—you must say his name aloud—my instinct to cover the mirror suggests a fear of being caught looking. If the Candyman can appear through my mirror, then my mirror—a formerly safe place to look—becomes a dangerous place where one cannot look without fear of being seen. This also brings to mind the idea of the monster as the woman's double—in this case, my own mirror image—an idea that seems to have roots in the trope of the human monster.

## HUMAN MONSTERS AND THE FEMINIZATION OF DISABILITY

The word "monster" was once a term used to refer to fetuses and human beings with deformities or physical disabilities.[9] As Fiedler notes, "'Monster' is as old as English itself, and remained the preferred name for Freaks[10] from the time of Chaucer to that of Shakespeare and beyond" (20). Now deemed an offensive term for human oddities, "monster" is most often associated with horror films and comic books. These monsters were the reason for Universal Studios' great success in the horror genre in the first half of the twentieth century. The term "Universal Monsters" refers to the long list of monster movies released by Universal from the early 1920s through to 1960 including *The Hunchback of Notre Dame* (1923), *Dracula* (1931), *Frankenstein* (1931), *The Mummy* (1932), and *The Phantom of the Opera* (1925). The films' monsters were not human oddities but entities such as werewolves, zombies, vampires, creatures, and other *things*.

Noel Carroll states that the monster in horror is incontestably threatening and dangerous, though not necessarily physically so. A monster that "kills and maims is enough" to satisfy this criteria; however, the monster may also pose a psychological, social, or moral threat to a society. For instance, it can destroy a person's identity, the moral order of a society, or advance an alternative society. Monsters can also trigger "enduring infantile fears, such as those of being eaten or dismembered, or sexual fears, concerning rape and incest." Carroll adds that monsters are also defined by their impurity, which is often seen in what he calls their "fusion." This is simply another way of saying that monsters shatter binaries, as do freaks, such as "inside/outside, living/dead, insect/human,

---

[9] See Chap. 1, pages 7–8 for a lengthier discussion of the use of the word "monster."

[10] Fiedler capitalizes the word "freak" throughout his study. I will not note this preference with *[sic]* repeatedly.

flesh/machine, and so on" (42–43). As the remainder of this chapter will illustrate, disabled bodies—both human and of the monster variety—are portrayed as monstrous bodies in horror. They pose either a physical or social threat and conflate binaries in ways that are always ambiguous and problematic.

Leslie Fiedler warns readers that they must not confuse these movie monsters with his "Freaks" or "Curiosities." As he says, "the freaky young do not [conflate the two]. Even stoned out of their minds at the latest horror show of some campus film series, or alone in their rooms watching the Fright Night feature on TV, they are aware that monsters are not 'real' as Freaks are" (23). Though he does not say so, Fiedler is in fact highlighting that by putting abnormal bodies on the screen in the form of monsters, a connection is being made between monsters and freaks. In other words, by warning us not to confuse the two, Fiedler assumes that one could confuse them, and that there is something monstrous about both the movie monster and the freak. Monsters, in his example, take the place of freaks, standing in as a neutralized version of a scary reality.

Horror allows us to confront otherness through the monster. A short passage from Katherine Dunn's novel *Geek Love* highlights this. Dunn's novel features a carny couple, Aloysius "Al" Binewski and his wife "Crystal" Lil, who use drugs and radiation during Crystal Lil's pregnancies in order to breed human oddities who they feel are superior to norms. Their children are: Arturo the Aquaboy, who has flippers instead of hands and feet; Olympia, an albino, hunchbacked dwarf who is considered the most normal of the siblings; Iphy and Elly, conjoined twin girls; and finally Chick, who is physically normal but has the gift of mind control.[11] In one scene, Arturo the seal boy talks to his sister, Olympia, about why he likes to read horror stories. He says that the stories do not scare him because the monsters in the stories—"written by norms to scare norms"—are just like him. He tells his sister: "We are the things that come to the norms in nightmares ... These books ... don't scare me because they're about me" (46). Arturo shows great insight here, paralleling the reactions he has caused in people with those of the victims in the horror stories he reads. He sees a monster in himself because others see a monster in him. Fiedler, however, sees a difference between freak

---

[11] See page 47, footnote 8.

and monster, and adamantly argues that, unlike the monster, the "true Freak" (such as Arturo),

> [s]tirs both supernatural terror and natural sympathy, since, unlike the fabulous monsters, he is one of us, the human child of human parents, however altered by forces we do not quite understand into something mythic and mysterious, as no mere cripple ever is. Passing either on the street, we may be simultaneously tempted to avert our eyes and to stare; but in the latter case we feel no threat to those desperately maintained boundaries on which any definition of sanity ultimately depends. Only the true Freak challenges the boundaries between male and female, sexed and sexless, animal and human, large and small, self and other, and consequently between reality and illusion, experience and fantasy, fact and myth. (24)

Fiedler denies that the monster in the pages of a book or on a screen can evoke the same fears and sympathies as a "true freak" can. This becomes complicated, however, when the monster on the screen is "one of us, the human child of human parents" as is, for example, Norman Bates. And Norman is not merely a human monster. Norman is a handsome (physically non-disabled and white), sympathetic, *likable* character who happens to do monstrous things. The product of a dysfunctional home life, Norman is as much sympathetic victim as he is monster. We root for him, wanting him to break free of his mother, and this fact does not change when we find out that Norman has assumed his mother's identity after murdering her. We are horrified at this fact, but we do not cease to see Norman as a human being. Even though Norman does become a physical horror in his cross-dressing, the one brief scene in which he appears in drag does not undo his physical normality. *Psycho* highlights horror's shift of focus from a supernatural monster to a human one. With this shift, horror forges an association between the monstrous body and monstrous acts.

This association is clearly depicted in *Rosemary's Baby*. If contact with the freak body is equated with horror, as it is in *Freaks*, then *Rosemary's Baby* also suggests that the pregnant body is both a horrible and freakish body. The film introduces us to Rosemary and Guy Woodhouse and follows the story of Rosemary's first pregnancy. Upon moving into their new home, Rosemary—after having been drugged and raped by her husband and their Satan-worshiping neighbors—becomes impregnated with the child of Satan himself. After becoming suspicious of her husband

and neighbors, Rosemary tries to flee in order to save her unborn baby and herself. She is brought home by her doctor, who believes her to be hysterical, and gives birth to the baby who is promptly taken from her, though Rosemary is told that the child dies. The film ends with Rosemary's decision to rock her baby's cradle and thus embrace her role as mother, even to a monstrous baby.

Almost as soon as she discovers that she is pregnant, Rosemary becomes nervous and fearful that something will go wrong with the pregnancy. She could certainly be described as hysterical, and she is quite paranoid at various points in the film. Lucy Fischer points to such worry and paranoia as healthy maternal bonding, and notes that it is normal for a woman to be fearful of her baby being born with an abnormality, for it to be "a monster, an idiot, [or] a cripple." Even if born healthy, the fetus while in utero can be seen as a type of parasite, draining its host (9–10). As viewers, we see the strain the pregnancy puts on Rosemary's body; it is in fact slowly killing her. It would not be a stretch, in other words, to say that the pregnancy has temporarily disabled her.

Rosemary's insistence that something is wrong with the baby is, of course, correct. Not only is he the spawn of Satan, but he is physically abnormal as we learn when Rosemary cries "What have you done to him? What have you done to his eyes, you maniacs?!" As her only comment on the baby's physical appearance, we can assume that he is otherwise normal except for his deformed eyes. The hybrid body of the infant brings to mind the half-man/half-animal (or half-woman or half-nonhuman, etc.) exhibits at the freak shows. The baby, half-human/half-demon, blurs the lines between what is and is not physically normal, as do the bodies on display at freak shows.

The film's central horror is found in the contact between Rosemary's body and the body of the freakish baby. Although the viewer does not see the baby's body on the screen, we do see the body of Rosemary as it grows and becomes grotesquely distorted throughout her pregnancy, or in other words, through contact with the freak body who, in this case, is literally growing inside her (see Fig. 3.1). Indeed, Rosemary's body is arguably the scariest and most abnormal image in the entire film. Waifish from the start, her body becomes simultaneously skeletal and swollen, her eyes sunken in, her small frame overwhelmed by her protruding pregnant stomach. An image of the pregnant Rosemary is not very different than, for example, one of Joseph Merrick, the Elephant Man. Just as the latter is a freak in the garb of a Victorian gentleman, so too is

**Fig. 3.1**  Rosemary's body in *Rosemary's Baby* (Polanski 1968)

Rosemary a misshapen, monstrous body in beautiful clothing and a chic hairstyle.

As *Rosemary's Baby* hints, the freak body is always displayed as a feminized body, even when biologically male. Through the staging of the body, the objectification of the body, and the dehumanization of the body, the body becomes characteristically female. Evidence lies in traditional female gender characteristics such as passivity, dependence, powerlessness, and vulnerability, all of which have historically been applied to freak show exhibits as well as the monstrous body in cinema. The horror film killer is often, as Clover notes, either "deformed, or dressed as a woman. Or 'he' *is* a woman" whom the audience was led to believe was male (such as in *Friday the Thirteenth I* [1980]). Such gender ambiguity is a constant throughout the horror genre. While many of horror's monsters may appear sexually potent and masculine—"the killer's phallic purpose, as he thrusts his drill or knife into the trembling bodies of women, is unmistakable"—his masculinity is almost always "severely disqualified" in his virginity, impotence, transvestitism, transsexuality, or literal womanhood. Even the "Terrible Place" in which the monster lives and/or attacks his victims is a decidedly vaginal space: dark, damp, and cavernous (Clover 44, 47–48).

As Diane Negra so plainly points out, "Behavior deemed 'monstrous' often involves crossing gender boundaries" (193). The disabled body in horror, like the monstrous female body, monsters, and monstrous killers, is decidedly feminized and spectacularized. Such a pattern is expected if we consider the fear of disability as well as the widespread ignorance regarding disability that exists in most societies. In other words, the pattern seems to be a way to suppress a fear of reproducing monstrosity. That the film industry would create disabled or monstrous bodies which are sexually impaired and therefore cannot procreate works through this fear. In horror, pregnancy becomes a disability; no one wants Rosemary to have another baby, after all. Eugenics suggests that the correct way to end social problems is through "selective breeding and the prohibition of breeding in certain cases (i.e., where a disability is present or a genetic link is detected)" (Accordino et al., 80).[12] In feminizing monstrous bodies, these horror films symbolically castrate the disabled male in order that he not procreate, thus putting the viewer at ease.

Both *Psycho* and *Rosemary's Baby* stage the fearful encounter at the border of freak and normal. This is true even in Norman's relationship to his mother's body; he becomes monstrous when his body and that of his mother's come into contact. While *Psycho* and *Rosemary's Baby* give us some insight into the human monster and the feminization of the freak body, they do not offer the opportunity for a reading of real disability because neither Norman nor Rosemary's bodies are disabled bodies in the true sense of the term. There are many horror movies that do, however, present disability in a more forthright way. One such film is Tobe Hooper's *The Texas Chainsaw Massacre*, a film that is in many ways *about* abnormal bodies. Its opening scene, which pictures decaying body parts,

---

[12] The fear of people with disabilities reproducing is a historic one; it was given a name, eugenics, in 1865 by Sir Francis Galton. In the mid-1890s, it was illegal in over half of America for people with disabilities—physical or intellectual—to marry. World War II saw the Nazi T-4 Euthanasia Program systematically "eradicate people with physical and intellectual disabilities through mass murder." Eugenics and euthanasia had their supporters in the USA as well. More recent high-profile instances such as Dr. Jack Kevorkian and Terry Shiavo have made it a very public and controversial issue that has left many Americans with disabilities "on edge" for fear that one day "society will offer euthanasia as an option to save a loved one with a serious disability from financial ruin, remove family members from stressful care giver roles, and as an option to cease being a financial burden on the state" (Accordino et al., 80–84).

hints as much; that one of its two central characters is a man in a wheel-chair only solidifies this fact.

The film tells the story of siblings Sally and Franklin Hardesty who travel with their friends, Jerry, Kirk, and Pam, to visit the Hardesty family's old abandoned home. What they don't know is that a nearby farm houses a family of men who once worked in the local slaughterhouse but who, because of industrialization, have become completely economically dispossessed and have been forced into cannibalism. The family consists of Grandpa, who looks like a corpse but still has a flicker of life in him; brothers, Hitchhiker and Leatherface, who do the killing for the family; and the Cook, who also works at the local gas station and who acts as a father figure to the brothers. The two "families" cross paths and one by one the teenagers are killed. Kirk, Pam, and Jerry are the first three to go; they are each brutally murdered by Leatherface as they enter the cannibal family's home. Franklin dies later, and Sally is the sole survivor.

The film is significant to examine because of the ways it parallels Franklin's disabled body with the grotesque bodies of the killers, Hitchhiker and Leatherface, but also because of its feminization and infantilization of both disabled and monstrous bodies. Franklin's disabled body is unattractive but it is not monstrous. However, it is aligned with the monstrous bodies of both Hitchhiker and Leatherface in ways that I will discuss below. This underscores the complex ways that the gaze is aligned with relative normality. It is not just about the viewer looking at monsters. It is about *looking*: watching people and monsters look at one another, monsters looking at each other, monsters looking at disabled bodies, disabled bodies looking at normal bodies, all looking back at the viewer. In other words, horror worries about destabilizing the border between normal and abnormal bodies and attempts to work through this with its focus on visual encounters.

Franklin's body—larger than his companions', wheelchair "bound," pale with dark hair—is strikingly different than the bodies which surround him. His sister and their friends are tall, slim, fair, able-bodied, and attractive. Their bodies are certainly on display through the men's tight clothing, revealing their strong, fit frames, and the girls' extremely scant clothing, revealing their slim, sexy bodies. Franklin's body, on the other hand, is neither strong nor sexy. The first time we meet him he is being rolled down a hill to urinate and his wheelchair tumbles over, a scene which highlights the baseness of the human body as well as Franklin's physical limitations. Scenes in the van show him sweaty and physically uncomfortable. That we are meant to view Franklin's body as grotesque, unattractive, and undesirable is clear. While we do not know the cause of Franklin's disability, we do know that he has had it since childhood, and that he is seen as a nuisance—an outsider who has been allowed to tag along to the party but not join in the fun.

Franklin's body is seen as a spectacle, and Franklin himself as a self-hating cripple. He is arguably the least happy character in the entire film, complaining about the weather, the group's activities, the decisions that are being made, and being isolated from the group. When he is left outside the house while the others run around exploring it, he mutters to himself and yells in an angry and bitter tone, slamming down on the wheels of his chair as he moves himself around. He is also an emasculated figure: he needs the care and assistance of the others in the film, is unable to get out of his chair (suggesting a lack of power as well as impotence), and is the only member of the group not in a sexual pairing.

Also significant in his emasculation is the opening scene in which he urinates. There is a pattern of referencing the disabled male's penis in horror—letting the viewer know that it exists and, in some capacity, functions—but later referencing that his penis is not used for sexual pleasure or is sexually dysfunctional. (We will see this again in my later discussions of both *The Funhouse* and *The Elephant Man*.) In Franklin's case, he is rolled down the hill and given a jar in which to urinate. As the camera pans away, the viewer's mind cannot help but picture Franklin aiming into the jar. In other words, Hooper forces the viewer to think about Franklin's penis and then throughout the film implies that even though he is biologically male, he does not use his penis and is thus symbolically female.

Franklin's fascination and contact with Hitchhiker illustrates the connection between Franklin's disability and monstrosity. Hitchhiker, with a long deep scar across his face, greasy hair, and twisted facial expressions, is clearly portrayed as freakish. In addition to his physical characteristics, he is freaked by his fascination with blood, death, and meat, his inability to behave appropriately in the social setting of the van, and of course his cannibalism. That he and Franklin are drawn to one another suggests that, as outsiders with physical differences, they see something of themselves in one another. This is clear when Hitchhiker takes Franklin's picture in the van. Pictures are taken to preserve memories or capture rare and interesting moments; thus the implication is that Hitchhiker is interested in and wants to preserve the sight of Franklin's body. However,

**Fig. 3.2** The Hitchhiker marks himself as freak; Franklin's look at the freak (*The Texas Chainsaw Massacre,* Hooper 1974)

when Franklin and the others reject him, refusing his dinner invitation and his offer to Franklin to buy his picture, he burns the picture and cuts Franklin's arm. Hitchhiker's sense of kinship with Franklin is shattered, and in rejecting his offers of friendship, Franklin reaffirms that he is not in fact like Hitchhiker. If Franklin is made a spectacle when he is photographed, then the destruction of the photograph breaks that illusion; however, the cutting of Franklin's body (and the promise of the scar it will leave behind) further mark Franklin as a spectacular and damaged body in a more permanent way than the photograph could. That Hitchhiker also cuts his own hand in this scene reinforces his and Franklin's shared freak identity, and Franklin's fascination that Hitchhiker could do that to himself—embrace his own freak status, freak himself—speaks to an acceptance of his body that Franklin does not have and that Hitchhiker fails to impart to Franklin (see Figs. 3.2 and 3.3). This marks Franklin's body as a transitional one; he is not quite freak but not quite normal either.

At its heart, *Texas Chainsaw* is a film about bodily suffering and trauma. Phillips argues that in *Texas Chainsaw,* "the world of the body is entirely devoid of spirit. It is

**Fig. 3.3** The Hitchhiker marks himself as freak; Franklin's look at the freak (*The Texas Chainsaw Massacre*, Hooper 1974)

animalistic savagery and sadism without an inkling of humanity" (116–117). While one certainly cannot dismiss the cannibalism or the brutal killings that take place in the family's home, I would argue that Leatherface's character is humane and is certainly not devoid of spirit. Similar to the decaying body parts seen at the film's opening, the house's bone room suggests that the ruined body is prized. Leatherface may destroy the human body through killing and eating it, but that does not mean that he does not see beauty or value in it, even after it has been ruined. Though many of the bones are strewn around on the floor, most of them have been crafted into furniture, decorations, and other household items. Though macabre, these items have been crafted by hand—Leatherface's. This suggests an artistry, the result of having taken great care with the materials. The bone room is an homage to the fractured body. Leatherface, its creator, like Hitchhiker, does what Franklin cannot—embrace the imperfect or "damaged" body.

One might also find parallels between Franklin and Leatherface, as the two are similar in weight and build (both are overweight and appear too large for their surroundings), and we could imagine that, if Franklin could stand, they would be about the same height as well. However, despite these physical similarities, when Leatherface wears his "killing mask" and wields his phallic chainsaw he is, unlike Franklin, all man. It is this masculinity and its implicit able-bodiedness, that allows him to kill Franklin so easily in the woods. Franklin's complete dependence on Sally and his inability to save himself are almost made comical by the awkward scene in which Sally struggles to get Franklin and his chair through the forest while Leatherface pursues them (of course, as the physically weaker of the pair, Franklin is the one to die). It is worth briefly noting that even though Franklin is the last male character to die, seemingly ranking him above the able-bodied men in the film, he only survives as long as he does because he is physically unable to wheel himself into the house where the others die. In fact, it is his exclusion from the group that keeps him safe throughout; he is only killed once he joins Sally. Unfortunately, in dying last he also suffers more than the other males in the film who die quick deaths and do not experience terrifying chase scenes in the woods.

Reminiscent of Norman Bates, Leatherface's identity seems to shift between masculine and feminine depending on which of his three masks he is wearing: his killing mask, his pretty woman mask, and his old woman mask. When not killing, his identity seems to be decidedly female. Likewise, the other male bodies in the film are domesticated, feminized bodies. Grandpa is too weak to perform the task of killing Sally. As the hammer falls from his hand, there is no doubt about his impotence and inability to finish the job. Similarly, the Cook tells us that he "can't take pleasure" in killing, another nod to sexual dysfunction. Leatherface and Hitchhiker are also infantilized during the dinner scene. Though both are adults, they are treated like naughty children by the Cook who yells at them and orders them around.

After Franklin is killed, the only "normal" body we see is Sally's,[13] and her body quickly becomes objectified and fractured. Like *Freaks*, *The Texas Chainsaw Massacre*'s key scene takes place at a ceremonial dinner. During this scene, the family sits around the dinner table in a sort of ritualistic preparation to kill, cook, and eat Sally. While no physical harm is being done to her at this point, the verbal promise of death pushes

---

[13] Hitchhiker has a facial disfigurement, Leatherface is monstrously large and wears grotesque masks, the Cook, though physically normal, is portrayed as evil through his dirtiness and ugliness, and Grandpa is grotesque—barely alive and, indeed, barely human.

her over the brink of hysteria. She begins screaming uncontrollably while her body is shattered—cut up—by the camera. First the camera zooms into her eye, to the point where she becomes unrecognizable. Then the camera flashes on various body parts and facial features. She cannot look away from the horror that is before her, and she herself becomes horrible to look at through the physical assault of the camera. She is simultaneously a victim, a viewer, and a monstrous body. Her body, once it is made spectacle, is also infantilized. In our final image of Sally, she is curled in a sitting fetal position in the back of a truck, covered in blood and crying—essentially an image of a fetus.

While *The Texas Chainsaw Massacre* clearly comments on the freakish body and suggests an alignment between disability, evil, and the grotesque, there is perhaps no other horror film that highlights the connection between horror and the carnival quite like another of Tobe Hooper's horror films, *The Funhouse*. The opening credits are interspersed with images of animatronic carnival figures: children, clowns, a fat lady, an old woman yielding a butcher's knife, and an executioner, among others. The movie begins in a bedroom where the viewer sees—through the eyes of the killer—many dark and sinister objects. As the killer stalks around the room we see a cage filled with mice, giant flies and spiders strewn about the room, and various scary masks and torture devices hanging from the walls. There is memorabilia from carnivals and monster and slasher films everywhere. Clearly, audiences are meant to believe that we are in the lair of a killer. His arm reaches out and grabs a large, rusty knife from the wall and then he slips a mask over his face. Our view is now limited, as we can only see what the killer sees out of the mask's two eye holes.[14] He stalks down the hallway where we know a teenage girl, Amy, has just stepped into the shower. A mock *Psycho*-style shower scene follows, from his point of view, in which Amy is "stabbed" by her younger brother's rubber knife. The viewer is quickly taken out of the horror and reassured that this is little kid stuff; there is nothing to be afraid of. Hooper, with such a dramatic opening, immediately and directly forges a connection for the viewer between the human monsters in films such as *Psycho* (the white male wielding a knife) and the monsters in films like *Frankenstein* (the memorabilia in the bedroom) with the carnivalesque freak show (the carnival figures that appear over the opening

---

[14] This is, of course, "borrowed" from *Halloween* (1978).

credits).[15] In a 2010 interview, Hooper says of the opening sequence that its purpose is to "immediately [let] you know you're watching a genre picture. In particular, too, it helped make the film a little safe. And I wanted that. Because I wanted the color and the fantasy, to build up to this moment where this person [who] is wearing a Frankenstein mask is actually the strange anomaly" (Hooper).

Hooper then brings us directly to the freak show. The rest of the movie takes place at a traveling carnival which Amy visits (against her better judgment) that night on a date with Buzz, her new boyfriend, Liz, her best friend, and Richie, Liz's goofy boyfriend. While at the carnival, the couples visit a freak show but human freaks are not exhibited; only freakish animals are on display (it is the 1980s after all—we can't exhibit freaks in freak shows, only horror movies; of course because this *is* a horror movie, we will confront the freak body in a different way). When Amy pulls her hand back from Daisy Mae, the two-headed cow, Richie teases her, "It's not gonna rub off on ya," reminding us that the able-bodied are often subconsciously afraid of abnormal bodies because they fear becoming disabled themselves. It is Richie, in fact, who is the most fascinated by the freaky animals, dragging the others into the must-see "feature attraction" of pickled punks. It is also Richie who puts the group in mortal danger, and he is punished for his transgressions as well as his interest in all things freaky—he is the first to die. Amy also seems to have a strange connection to the carnival, although she does not necessarily seem to enjoy it as Richie does. There are three odd moments in the film where Amy is drawn to meet the gaze of three carnival workers in prolonged stares: the freak show barker, the funhouse operator, and the girlie show barker (all played by the same actor, Kevin Conway). These moments, which abruptly interrupt the film's action, serve to reinforce the difference between Amy's normalcy and the freakishness of the carnival because norm and freak are directly entered into a stare.

The horror does not take place until the carnival shuts down for the night. Hooper makes it a point to show the lights slowly going out, the crowd dispersing, and the rides stopping. The camera pans over the carnival grounds and reveals that the only people left are the carnies. Not all

---

[15] Diane Negra's article, "Coveting the Feminine: Victor Frankenstein, Norman Bates, and Buffalo Bill," puts Frankenstein and Bates in direct conversation, as seen in her title. Negra provides an excellent Freudian reading of the ambiguous gender identities represented in the three texts.

are freaks, of course; in fact, we only see one or two typical freak show bodies, but, because all of the able-bodied, non-carnival workers are leaving, we get the sense that we are very clearly somewhere we are not supposed to be. The viewer does not belong here anymore than Amy and her friends do. As the camera returns to the dark funhouse, where the group has decided to camp out for the night, the viewer knows that they will be punished for trespassing into the world of the carnival.

It is here that Amy and her friends discover that Gunther, the son of the funhouse's barker, Conrad, lives in the basement below the ride. We know very little about Gunther, just that he helps his father operate the ride, he always wears a Frankenstein's monster mask, and he never speaks. We see Gunther a few times before this, though in seemingly insignificant shots. After leaving the girlie show, for instance, Gunther walks past them and the guys make fun of him while Amy comments on how strange he is. Buzz jokes that it "looks like old Frankenstein has to get his jollies also." This scene foreshadows what the group later witnesses in the funhouse.

During the night, the group hears voices coming from below them. Peering through the floorboards, they watch Gunther as he engages Madame Zena, the fortune teller, as a prostitute. While it is unusual for the freakish body to be displayed as a sexually active body, Gunther certainly fits the profile of the sexually dysfunctional body. The two do not have sex; Madame Zena gives him a handjob and while he does ejaculate, he does so prematurely (all while wearing his *Frankenstein* mask). It is unclear whether this is what he paid her for or whether it was meant as a prelude to intercourse. Regardless, Gunther responds with embarrassment and anger over his premature ejaculation, demanding that Zena return the hundred dollars he paid her. When she refuses, he chokes her to death. The rest of the plot centers on Gunther and Conrad discovering that the teens witnessed the murder. The characters are killed off one by one: Conrad kills Richie, Gunther kills Liz, Buzz kills Conrad, Gunther kills Buzz, Gunther chases Amy and then accidentally kills himself. Amy is the only survivor—another final girl.

It is interesting that the viewer only sees Gunther without his Frankenstein mask after he fails as a sexual partner and is thus emasculated. Up until this point, the viewer does not know what he looks like underneath the mask, but he seems scary because of the presence of the monster mask. He is emasculated but then immediately asserts his masculinity by killing Zena, and the viewer is horrified. When the mask is removed, however, we realize that the movie monster (in this case, Frankenstein's monster) is harmless in comparison to the true horror of the deformed body. Gunther is truly hideous. His facial deformities are difficult to describe, but Hooper has said in interviews that he has a "cleft head" (Hooper). His red eyes are set quite far apart and he has a severe cleft palate that seems to travel up his entire face. His mouth is large, has fangs, and is dripping with copious amounts of drool. The viewer cannot help but be horrified at the sight of him. Within the context of the film, Fiedler's earlier point that movie monsters cannot be confused with real freaks seems accurate. The monster mask literally hides a much scarier reality. Of course, in choosing a monster mask, Hooper connects the movie monster with the monstrous body and, like *Freaks*, reinforces the connection between freakish bodies and morally corrupt deeds. This also reasserts, once again, that at the center of horror is not the monster, but the viewer's fear of contact with the monstrous body.

Ultimately, the film makes a comment on the helplessness of the freak body. The freak animals, for example, are on display and can do nothing about it. Upon viewing a cow with a cleft palate (clearly foreshadowing Gunther's freakishness) and the two-headed cow in the freak show, Amy comments on how sad the animals look. We are, of course, meant to make a connection between these animals and Gunther who, wild and without speech, seems very much an animal himself. Though they are frightening, we are meant to pity both the animals and Gunther. Hooper urges us to realize that, like Hans in *Freaks*, they may be different, but they have feelings. During the scene between Gunther and Zena, we cannot help but feel sorry for him, especially after he kills her and realizes what he's done. He beats himself and hides in the corner while Conrad yells at him and talks him into killing the kids upstairs. It is clear that Gunther only "takes care of the problem" reluctantly, after being sweet-talked by Conrad who reassures Gunther that he will take care of him and that the sound of Gunther's "voice" doesn't scare him.[16] That we are to pity Gunther is made even more apparent when he kills Liz. As he approaches her, Liz offers sex in exchange for her life, telling him, "I can make you

---

[16] As in *Texas Chainsaw*, Gunther is a freak killer who does the bidding of a father figure. The presence of the morally corrupt father figure misguiding or mistreating the childlike freak is a common trope, also seen in *The Elephant Man*.

feel good." Gunther seems willing to accept her affection; he hugs her and strokes her hair, clearly starved for any kind of human connection. He only ends up killing her because she stabs him, rejecting his affection.[17]

Tobe Hooper's monstrous freaks in *The Texas Chainsaw Massacre* and *The Funhouse* are self-hating, powerless, animalistic, and/or sexually dysfunctional. While the viewer does experience a certain amount of pity for characters like Franklin, Leatherface, and Gunther, such feelings are only secondary to disgust or fear. Even in *Freaks*, the viewer is ambivalent because the freaks are as guilty as Cleopatra. These examples illustrate that the freakish bodies we see in horror are not merely scary to look at. They are scary in our connection with them—they can touch and be touched, they can be human and engage in the same everyday activities that we can, and even when they do horrible things, they are still capable of feeling sadness, empathy, and loneliness. Viewers imagine that the monster can almost be normal and can also picture themselves being almost monstrous. We are reminded of the blurry distinction between normal and freak bodies which is in itself horrific.

## INSPIRATION AND PITY IN THE DISABILITY DRAMA

The poster child of the charity telethon is never horrific, never grotesque, never severely physically disabled. He or she may use crutches or a wheelchair for mobility, but will otherwise be as cute and normal looking as any average child. Many of us can picture an adorable child dressed in fine clothes, on crutches, perhaps, or with some other non-threatening disability, achieve the miraculous and take a few steps, or smile and tell us how much he or she loves life. It is an image that pulls on the heartstrings of America and, most importantly to the producers of such images, opens wallets. This child is a symbol that has long been inspiring and uplifting for the non-disabled and has prompted immense generosity from a large number of people. However, for the disabled community, the poster child is a loathed symbol of pity that has done much more harm than good. It is so damaging because it encourages the notion that people with disabilities are "childlike, dependent, and in need of charity

---

[17]This mirrors the scene in *Texas Chainsaw* in which Hitchhiker is rejected by Franklin. In this parallel, the disfigured Hitchhiker is the monster and the disabled Franklin the feminized victim.

or pity." In other words, telethons and their poster children send the message that the disabled need the help of the non-disabled and that if they donate enough money "the disabled children"—and thus disability itself—"will go away." Shapiro points to the fact that there are never poster adults, only children. He argues that this sends the message that disability is intolerable and unmentionable in adults, but that people could deal with "cute and innocent children" (15).

With the polio vaccination came the belief that disability was conquerable, that it did not have to be a permanent condition if the disabled person would just work hard enough at becoming "the flipside of the pitiable poster child," but is "just as hurtful" because "it implies that a disabled person is presumed deserving of pity—instead of respect—until he or she proves capable of overcoming a physical or mental limitation through extraordinary feats" (16). The "supercrip" or inspirational disabled person is, in other words, a trope that sees people with disabilities as inspirational for doing everyday tasks that, were it not for the individual's functional limitations, would not be seen as extraordinary. This is problematic because most people with disabilities cannot simply work through their limitations and make themselves ablebodied through hard work and determination. This also assumes that everyone with a disability would "correct it" if they could, an assumption that, according to Cyndi Jones, a former poster child, is equivalent to assuming that all black people would make themselves white if they could (12–14, 16).

These tropes have been played out in many different versions and through many different platforms, including a genre of film that often borders on horror but is not

categorized or marketed as such. I am opting to call this genre "disability melodrama," a type of melodrama in which the main character is disabled and in which the pity paradigm is strong. Linda Williams characterizes melodrama as "a peculiarly democratic and American form that seeks dramatic revelation of moral and emotional truths through a dialectic of pathos and action." Further, she argues:

If emotional and moral registers are sounded, if the work invites us to feel sympathy for the virtues of beset victims, if the narrative trajectory is ultimately more concerned with a retrieval and staging of innocence than with the psychological causes of motives and action, then the operative mode is melodrama. In cinema the mode of melodrama defines a broad category of moving pictures that move us to pathos for protagonists beset by forces more powerful than they and who are perceived as victims. Since the rise of American melodrama on the mid-nineteenth century stage, a relatively feminized victimhood has been identified with virtue and innocence. ("Melodrama Revised" 42)

Melodrama engages the viewers' sympathies by victimizing its protagonists through means greater than them or through no fault of their own, and focuses on redeeming or saving the victimized protagonist rather than exploring their situation in any meaningful way. Further, through such "virtuous suffering" and punishment, the melodrama protagonist is aligned with the monstrous body and yet retains the viewers' identification, particularly when the protagonist is disabled. This subgenre of melodrama follows a distinct pattern in which the viewer is told the story of an often male protagonist with a disability who is at first frightful or pitiable, and we watch as he is cured or cures himself, is accepted into nondisabled society, or comes to terms with his or her disability and thus becomes morally healed. More often than not, this protagonist does not survive and thus disability melodramas do not offer a solution but just a fantasy conciliation.

There have been many films of this breed spanning across decades, subgenres of drama, and gender and racial boundaries. The story of New York Yankees' great Lou Gehrig, *The Pride of the Yankees* (1942), downplays Gehrig's impressive career while emphasizing the sadness of his disease. *My Left Foot* (1989) tells the story of Christy Brown, a man with cerebral palsy who only has control over his left foot, but overcomes this limitation, becoming a painter and a writer. In *The Horse Whisperer* (1998), Scarlett Johansson plays a young girl who is in a horseback riding accident which causes her leg to be partially amputated and her horse to become disabled. Her parents take them to a horse healer, and both are rehabilitated. In *The Bone Collector* (1999), Lincoln Rhyme, an ex-cop who has become a quadriplegic, is planning on having an assisted suicide when he hears of terrible crimes being committed in his neighborhood and his will to live is renewed through helping others. Perhaps no other disability drama is more famous than *The Miracle Worker* (1962), the story of Helen Keller, born blind, deaf, and mute, who is miraculously taught to communicate by Anne Sullivan, also visually impaired. These are just a few of the many films that play on the viewer's pity and as a result reinforce negative views of people with disabilities.

David Lynch's 1980 film *The Elephant Man* is a keystone example of this narrative. Though there were many disability pity dramas before it, the genre saw a tremendous rise in popularity after its release. Though this may be mere coincidence, *The Elephant Man* remains one of the most complex and, in many ways, beautiful films of its kind. It certainly adds much to the discourse on the portrayal of the freakish body and the history of cinematic representations.

*The Elephant Man* is based on the true story of a nineteenth century freak performer, Joseph Merrick (1862–1890), whom the movie fictionalizes as John Merrick, a man with severe body and facial deformities. Merrick joined the sideshow in his twenties, and although true-life accounts vary, the movie's version is that he lived a life not far removed from slavery while under the care of his sideshow manager Bytes, who claims Merrick as his possession and treats him as if he were an animal. Merrick is eventually rescued by and brought under the care of Dr. Frederick Treves who obtains a permanent home for Merrick in the London hospital (Durbach 33–34). The film follows Merrick on his journey from sideshow freak to medical specimen, and finally to the life of a respected Victorian gentleman. Though the real Merrick's medical diagnosis has changed since his lifetime, it seems to now be the common belief that he had Proteus syndrome, characterized by the following: "macrocephaly; hyperostosis of the skull; hypertrophy of long bones; and thickened skin and subcutaneous tissues, particularly of the hands and feet, including plantar hyperplasia, lipomas, and other unspecified subcutaneous masses" (Tibbles 683). It is worth noting that John Hurt, who plays Merrick in the film, is not disabled.

The basic plot certainly plays on the pity paradigm, casting Merrick as a childlike cripple in need of rescuing. Of course, the freak show performer cast as a miserable slave is not altogether historically untrue; however, this was not a dominant trend. Many freak show performers were well paid, self-sufficient, and enjoyed what they did.[18] To portray Merrick as suffering and abused allows the audience to pity him and to see him as human. In keeping with his childlike qualities, when Treves

---

[18] For example, the documentary *Sideshow: Alive on the Inside!* (1999) provides numerous interviews with ex-sideshow performers including Percilla the Monkey Girl who says "what could be more fun for a child" than being raised at the circus? Similarly, Jeanie the Half-Girl loved being a sideshow freak because people paid attention to her and brought her gifts and she was able to be the main financial supporter of her family.

does "rescue" Merrick from the freak show, he is portrayed as unintelligent and unable to communicate, although in keeping with the qualities of melodrama, he is later revealed to be rather sophisticated and intelligent. When the audience hears him speak for the first time, both Treves and the audience are humbled when we suddenly recognize Merrick as human.

It is important to point out that as these initial scenes set up the larger story, the viewer does not see Merrick's body. Instead, audiences are shown how to look or what to expect through the looks of others on the screen. In other words, we see other characters in the film look and react to Merrick with frightened screams, essentially building the suspense and telling us to be afraid of what to expect when we do see him. By the time we do see Merrick's body, we are very curious indeed. This is a popular ploy of the freak show—audiences are teased with posters and barkers who build excitement for the exhibit so that audiences are on edge even before they enter the exhibit. In *The Elephant Man*, we receive a mixed message, however, because when Treves sees Merrick he does not scream, nor does he gasp in horror. He cries. This response tells the viewer that while most are frightened of Merrick's appearance, there is something tragic in it. Treves, being a man of science and stereotypically on the cold and unfeeling side, moves us and we are apt to want to receive Merrick as he does, with compassion and pity.

Our fear of Merrick's disability is neutralized in two other ways. The first is simply that once the viewer does see him, we look at so much of his body so often. Indeed, throughout the film we look at Merrick's body more than any other body. We watch him sleep, groom, interact with others, and create artwork; we see him watching others and watching the world around him; and we watch him being looked at by countless others, their expressions softening from fear to pity as the film progresses. This excessive looking serves to familiarize the viewer with the freakish body, essentially breaking a key rule of the freak show: the more you let audiences see, the less curious they will be.

Our fear is also assuaged by the feminization of Merrick. As Linda Williams has argued, we find the human body freakish when it is comprised of "too much or too little" of something. In Merrick's case, he has too much of everything: too much bone, too much skin, and too large a head, hands, and feet. In horror, having too much physically, according to Williams, means being sexually exaggerated. As she notes, "it is a truism of the horror genre that sexual interest resides most often in the monster and not the bland ostensible heroes" ("When the Woman Looks" 20). In order to neutralize this, he needs to be feminized. Much like Franklin and Gunther, the viewer is told that Merrick has normal and functional genitalia. While the viewer sees much of his body, we do not see his genitals; however, a room full of male scientists in the film do when Treves uses him as a specimen in a lecture. It is noteworthy that this is one look that is not returned. In other words, when the true "freak show" is fully revealed the audience does not get to see it. We only see the look *at* the freak show—the faces of the scientists as they gaze upon Merrick's naked body.

It is significant that the viewer is aware that Merrick has normal genitals because this knowledge allows us to feminize him when he doesn't use them. As a freak, he is already in a feminized position—all freaks, because they are not in control of the gaze, are in a female subject position. As Williams and Clover have argued, horror's monsters often appear sexually exaggerated, but are eventually shown to be impotent or otherwise sexually powerless. It is this that equates the monster as the woman's double. However, unlike in horror, there is no illicit sexuality here. Merrick is not sexually dysfunctional as Gunther is. Instead he is completely lacking sexuality like Franklin. Thus, under the guise of the scientific gaze, horror structures the unused penis as a means to feminize the disabled body for purposes of sympathy. The film makes it a point to let the viewer know that Merrick has the ability to fuck, but that he doesn't (and doesn't even try to) underscores his innocence and of course lessens our fears of the monstrous offspring he might be capable of producing.

Merrick's identification with his mother also speaks to this feminization. His mother was a normal, beautiful woman who died young. The film, through a series of flashback images, shows Merrick's mother being frightened by an elephant while pregnant, thus implying maternal impression, a long discredited medical theory that explained the presence of birth defects by accrediting them to psychological or emotional trauma suffered by the mother while pregnant. This implicates the mother in the child's disability, though even more so implies that disability is out of our control, a result of happenstance or outside influences. Merrick carries his mother's picture with him and obsesses over her image. Of his father, we know nothing. However, because we cannot possibly imagine someone as beautiful as Merrick's mother birthing a monstrosity, we are led to believe that Merrick's father must then be the "elephant" or the monstrosity in him. In other words, it is the male part of him that is monstrous. To get closer to the feminine (reconnect with his dead mother), he must escape the masculine (overcome his disability as well as escape from the paternal figure of Bytes). Though the film tries to assure us that this is possible for Merrick, it is ultimately ambivalent about whether he is able to transcend his disability. The film's penultimate scene in which Merrick visits the theater speaks to this. Merrick has, at this point in the film, been accepted into London society: he dresses like a gentleman, has prestigious and notable visitors, and is given fine gifts. When Treves brings him to the theater, he knows Merrick is dying. Mrs. Kendall, the famous actress who has befriended Merrick and who stars in the play, dedicates the performance to Merrick and he receives a standing ovation from the crowd.

The scene in which Merrick watches the play is one of visible deformation. The initial impression is that Merrick is no longer a freak because he is no longer on the stage—he is no longer performing freak, but is a viewer just like everyone else. He is now a member of the audience looking at the performance through a normalized gaze. It would seem that his entrance into normal life is gained through shared looking with others. It would be incorrect, however, to categorize Merrick as the crowd's equal because he does not, in fact, have access to the normal gaze. We know this because, first, we see through Merrick's freaked gaze. The camera allows us access to a normalized view of the stage, Merrick's view of the stage (we see it as he sees it), and a view of Merrick's face as he watches the stage. When we see the stage, it appears as a normal play. However, when we look at Merrick looking, a distorted image of the stage appears overlapping his face. Finally, when we see the stage through Merrick's eyes—when we see what the freak sees—the images become completely distorted. He sees the actors and props in duplicate and triplicate, they blur as they overlap and move closer and then further away, and the images move in slow motion. So although Merrick has presumably gained access to normality—he is able to look and to see beautiful and sophisticated things—his "normal" gaze is freaked (Figs. 3.4 and 3.5).

Second, despite the fact that Merrick is indeed looking, he is still being looked at by us, the viewer of the film. In other words, we need to see him to see that he is looking—our look at the freak is inescapable. His status of perpetual freak is confirmed when the audience applauds him instead of the actors onstage because they are applauding him for

**Fig. 3.4** The normal gaze. What the viewer sees when they look at the stage in *The Elephant Man* (Lynch 1980)

**Fig. 3.5** The freak gaze. What Merrick sees when he looks at the same image in *The Elephant Man* (Lynch 1980)

no other reason than his freak status. He has done nothing but put on a suit and attend a show, just like all the other men in the audience. Merrick has become the "worthy cripple" whose role it is to inspire the non-disabled.

Merrick cannot even escape his freak role in death, although the film visually suggests that he does. Once he has taught Treves and the greater society a lesson about humanity, his role as a disabled compass of morality—and as an object of inspiration porn (picked up in Chap. 5)—is completed. He has been melodramatically sacrificed. Merrick's death, in the film, is a choice that he makes for himself. While it can be argued that he chooses his death at this particular time because he has been accepted to Victorian society and has reached the pinnacle of his life's happiness, the theater scene weighs heavily on this transcendence. A controlled, solitary death may be the closest thing to transcendence for Merrick—a sad statement, indeed, that the only way to escape his freak identity is to kill himself. Sadder still is that death has *not* been an escape for the real Merrick whose skeleton was exhibited for many years at the London Hospital Medical College (images of it are widely available on the internet) and whose life has remained under public scrutiny.[19]

Lynch's portrayal of Merrick as first an object of pity and then a source of inspiration, as well as other similar representations, are damaging because they are "internalized by disabled and nondisabled people alike and build social stereotypes, create artificial limitations, and contribute to the discrimination and minority status hated by most disabled people" (Shapiro 30). While it seems contradictory to say that we should not look at someone like Merrick as a brave and inspirational man, it is problematic in the condescension and oppression that often lie behind such praise. Indeed, the supercrip paradigm is a limiting and unrealistic view of the lives of those with disabilities, and it overshadows the constant daily struggles of the disabled, such as access and equality, which are in desperate need of visibility to begin with.

## Bringing Back *Freaks*

As I argued at the beginning of this chapter, *Freaks* brought the freak show from the carnival to the movies, a transference that has had a significant effect on cinema, notably in the genres of horror and disability melodrama. *Freaks* was not a direct representation of the freak show, but a cinematic interpretation that allowed a different kind of access to the freakish body. In seating audiences in a theater, *Freaks*, as well as the horror films that followed, succeeded in simultaneously bringing freaks and

---

[19] Odd rumors abound on the internet about how Michael Jackson was obsessed with Merrick and tried to buy his skeleton from the London Hospital for an undisclosed amount in the 1980s. Whether factual or mere rumor, this struck me an interesting example of how a self-made freak tends to identify with a "born freak."

norms closer together on screen, while distancing freaks and norms in this space of spectatorship. The medium of film rejects the freak show format and, because the freaks can not look back, the freak-norm relationship is challenged, though it is not eradicated. Rather, these films attempt to work out the problematic relationship between different bodies, allowing audiences a physical distance in the theater that is essential to facilitating self-reflection in viewing the freakish body on a screen.

I do not mean to suggest that the freakish body can only be confronted in a darkened theater. However, I do believe that the medium of film can and has served as a conduit for viewers to work through their reactions to freakish bodies. *Freaks* has been the most successful film in provoking ambivalent yet thoughtful responses to the portrayal of the freak in film and, further, the ethics in looking at the freak. With its suggested sexuality, theatrical representations of freakish bodies, and reluctance to show audiences any more than necessary, the freak show offered a highly mediated, spectacularized interpretation of otherness. *Freaks* certainly offers a highly mediated, carnivalesque spectacle as well. However, unlike its successors, *Freaks* generally does not fall prey to damaging paradigms of disability such as the supercrip or pity paradigms, and when viewers do feel inspired by or pity for the characters with disabilities, it is because actions and circumstances have warranted such responses, not because they are disabled. While *Freaks* is not perfect in resisting such paradigms, it is largely more successful than the other films I have discussed. Almost all of the scholarship on *Freaks* reads the film adversely, but I believe that in doing so many are buying into injurious tropes about people with disabilities.

For example, many have criticized the "stiff, self-conscious performances" of the film's cast. The "wooden delivery" of their lines leaves much to be desired and may keep audiences from becoming immersed in the drama. The drama, described as "contrived," is also panned. Rachel Adams calls the plot a "thin story of love and vengeance that makes a flimsy pretext" for gathering the group of freaks together on film (67). It is an unusual case, indeed, that most members of the cast were not actors used to speaking, but freaks who were used to being stared at. That they are often stiff and awkward keeps us aware that we are watching a film, and thus keeps us aware of our own presence in the theater and thus our own bodies, allowing for self-reflection. Further, the admittedly awkward introductions serve a larger, more important purpose. Much like our excessive looks at Merrick's body in *The Elephant Man*, these early scenes allow us to get used to looking at difference and thus act as an invitation into their lives.

I have argued that *Freaks* was progressive in its view of people with disabilities as healthy, sexual beings. The film, while forcing the viewer to consider the erotic possibilities of freakish sexual pairings, nevertheless also forces us to realize that freakish bodies are not broken or incapable of human love and affection. An example is found in the scene in which the Bearded Lady gives birth to the Walking Skeleton's child. Another character leans over and asks her, "What is it?" When most people ask a new mother "what is it?" we expect the answer to either be "a boy" or "a girl." The joke here is that the phrase is a tongue-in-cheek nod to a famous freak show advertisement that anyone familiar with the history of the freak show would recognize. One of P.T. Barnum's most famous freak performers, a man with microcephaly (commonly known as a pinhead), was famously billed as "Zip, the What Is It?" The scene plays out like an inside joke of the freak show. That it is also a comic moment that pokes fun at the fear of procreation by freaks (which I have discussed throughout this chapter), speaks to *Freaks'* attempt to neutralize and normalize the freakish body. It also treats freak sexuality as not simply something subversive or shocking, but something lighthearted and ordinary.

In her reading of *Freaks*, Adams points out the film's many contradictory statements in its message: freaks are seen as both innocent children and lewd adults; freaks belong in nature but they are freaks of nature; freaks are asexual but they are overly sexual at the same time (69–75). I would respond that the contradictions imbedded in the film attempt to move beyond stereotypical classifications of freakish bodies. While *Freaks* does not set out to show a true-to-life portrayal of disability, and while its plot may be somewhat outlandish, it offers a more realistic view of disability than its horror successors. While I do not mean to suggest that *Freaks* was successful in normalizing the freak body, I am asserting that if cinema insists on using the freak body as a metaphor, then at least *Freaks* does so in positive and progressive ways.

The box-office failure of *Freaks* made honest representations of disability a difficult tradition to carry on, and the films that succeed it do so as alternative representations to those in *Freaks*. Everything that *Freaks* was panned for has been shifted in post-1960s horror and disability melodrama. If *Freaks* is not the freak show, but an interpretation of it, then the horror movies and melodramas which I have discussed are not the freak show either, nor are they working quite in the tradition of *Freaks*. Rather, they work in an odd anti-tradition, keeping away from the boldness and "indecency" of *Freaks* and finding alternative ways to present freakishness that, while less honest and more prey to damaging cultural perceptions of disability, still embrace the spirit of *Freaks* and the freak show itself. With the normalizing gaze, the fear of contact with the freak, the sexual narratives surrounding the freak body, the backstories of abuse, and the sympathetic characterizations of the monstrous, horror defines the freak body in relation to normal activity while asserting that we still see and think about the freak body as abnormal.

## CHAPTER 4

# Reality, Normality, Sexuality: "Authentic" Portrayals of the Freak

Robert Bogdan tells us that because the freak show has been considered lewd, exploitative, shocking, and a "practice on the margin" that is only viewed by people with questionable morals, it has been referred to by some as the "pornography of disability" (2). There *is* something implicitly pornographic about the freak show, particularly highlighted in the staging of freakish bodies in ways that suggest subversive sexuality. The scenes in *Freaks*, for example, in which the conjoined Daisy and Violet Hilton interact with their husbands are pornographic because they illustrate that the sexual pleasure of both twins is up for grabs when only one is engaged in sexual activity. By most standards, this is considered lurid, lewd, and sensational—characteristics of both the freak show and pornography.

While there may be something merely suggestive of the pornographic in many freak show portrayals, nowhere is it clearer (except, of course, in actual pornography, as I will discuss in the following chapter) than in portrayals of the freak body that label themselves as real: documentaries, reality television, docuseries, and talk shows. The idea that the freak show is the "pornography of disability" does speak to a central concern of the freak show, new and old; that is, the search for access to the (authentic, sexual) freak body.

The traditional freak show claimed to exhibit real-life freaks, and the narratives that went along with these exhibits were advertised as being true even though the stories and, at times, the bodies themselves, were often exaggerated or even outright fictional. In this discussion,

© The Author(s) 2017                                                              79
J.L. Williams, *Media, Performative Identity, and the New American Freak Show*, DOI 10.1007/978-3-319-66462-0_4

I am not concerned necessarily with the actual authenticity of the freak body (though I will take this topic up in the next chapter), but with the moniker of "real-life" to refer to the bodies on display. Why do we want to see what "shouldn't" be seen? What does it mean for the viewer to watch a true-life account of a freak body, rather than one you know or even suspect might be fictional? Do we see the body differently when we are told it is real?

André Bazin states that photography and cinema "satisfy ... our obsession with realism" because they are more than imitations of this world; they are the world "re-presented, set before us, that is to say, in time and space" (13–14). Linda Williams, deliberating Bazin's ontology of the photographic image, argues that this realism "lead[s] directly, then, to obscenity," a point Bazin makes elsewhere himself ("Power, Pleasure, and Perversion" 37). Williams reasons that viewers become complicit in the acts that we view on screen despite our spatial and temporal separation from those images (38). The distance between object and viewer allows the latter to simultaneously participate but detach and, thus, take no responsibility for the things viewed. Therefore, the distance implicit in film, and, by extension, television, should allow for access to more intimate moments with freak bodies than the traditional freak show offered.

As the weird history of snuff films illustrates, the viewing public has a perverse fascination with seeing a real depiction of what shouldn't be seen. The voyeuristic desire for a behind-the-scenes moment speaks to a cultural fascination with death and sex and the conflation of the two. The popular legend of snuff is that it originated with the supposed circulation of South American films which showed "'women who were killed on camera as the gruesome climax to sexual acts' [which] had been confiscated by police" (Hagin 44–45). The 1976 film *Snuff* purported to do this very thing; it ends with a realistic depiction of the dismemberment and disembowelment of a woman. Not surprisingly, "the idea of snuff continued to haunt the [public's] imagination" even after the sensational film was revealed to be a hoax (45).[1]

Linda Williams suggests that the fascination with snuff can be traced to the intersection of the "spectacles of pleasure ... and pain." Williams

---

[1] Hagin suggests that there is a longer and much more complex history behind snuff films. What I recount here is the most basic and commonly told origin of snuff.

continues that what is "particularly disturbing" about snuff is "the sense in which an involuntary spasm of pain culminating in death becomes imaginable as a substitute for the *invisible* involuntary spasm of [female] orgasm" ("Power, Pleasure, and Perversion" 42). This desire to make the unseen seen is not unique to snuff films. The existence of disability pornography such as stump and midget porn, discussed at greater length in the next chapter, also suggests that people desire to see what is off-limits or unspeakable—what was previously unseen, merely provoked by the freak show, now becomes visible. The discomfort, disgust, and obscenity that are associated with the sexuality of people with disabilities come, perhaps, from the fact that sexuality and disability contradict one another. To actively engage in sexual activity suggests control over one's body, identity, and gender, agencies which are not freely ascribed to people with disabilities. Therefore, to think of someone with a freakish body engaging in a sex act seems off-limits and obscene, and to watch it is even more subversive.

In the traditional freak show, subversive sexuality and gender are almost always suggested, implied but never directly discussed. The obvious sexual oddities of the freak show—bearded ladies, hermaphrodites, men and women with malformed genitals—call into question the common belief in the bipolarity of the sexes, yet never explicitly reveal their sexual difference to audiences. Similarly, conjoined twins arouse curiosities about freak sexuality as Fiedler observes when he writes, "joined twins have evoked erotic fantasies in their audience, since they suggest inevitably the possibility of multiple fornication—or at least the impossibility of sexual privacy" (206). For instance, the conjoined twins, Chang and Eng Bunker, were routinely pictured with their combined 21 children, which illustrates that the freak show can hint at, but not directly show us freak sexuality and gender identity.

*Geek Love* can, and does, move beyond the freak show perhaps because reading is an imaginative rather than a visual experience. Perhaps Dunn was thinking of Chang and Eng when she decided to explore the sexuality of the conjoined twins Iphy and Elly.[2] When the twins decide to allow men to have sex with them for money, the reader is conflicted because Iphy does not want to give up her virginity. Elly explains her

---

[2] Iphy and Elly have separate torsos, arms, and heads, but share one body from the waist down. To have sex with one of them would be to have sex with both of them.

decision: "'You know what the norms really want to ask?…What they want to know, all of them, but never do unless they're drunk or simple, is How we fuck? That and who, or maybe what. Most of the guys want to know what it would be like to fuck us. So I figure, why not capitalize on that curiosity?" (207). The girls sell their virginity and continue to allow men to have sex with them for money. After their initial sexual experience, it is unclear for the reader—and the girls' sexual partner—whether or not Iphy was raped even though Elly gave consent. As the man who buys their virginity says, "I don't think I was right. I think I did something…wrong. One of them didn't want it. She cried and scratched at me. The other one…did" (393). This scene lifts the veil of the freak show and shows viewers (or, in this case, readers) what is on the minds—whether consciously or not—of people who would have viewed conjoined twins in the freak show. As previously noted, the freak show hints at the perverse sexuality of conjoined twins; here, Dunn explores it in an uncompromising and unfiltered way. The conflict Dunn explores in this scene speaks to the particular sexual fascination with conjoined twins, but, more generally, also of the sexual fascination with freaks in general. Audiences want to see the real rather than what is staged; they want to peek behind the curtain.

In what follows, I argue that television series attempt but fail to reach similar moments. We have seen the freak show move away from the spectator in both space and time—film physically and temporally distanced freak from spectator—while we have watched the borders of freak and norm become ambiguous onscreen. Through real-life portrayals, whose primary media is television, we move closer still to Bahktin's notion of the carnivalesque. In other words, the freakish spectacle, in its appropriation of the term "reality" or "real-life," moves further from an artistic form and clings instead to the "borderline between art and life" (Bakhtin 6). "Reality television" portrayals are not true-life, but are not fiction either. These blurred lines begin to move the freak body back into the real world and undo the distance created by the freak body's movement to film.

Like both the traditional freak show and film, television needs audiences to function; audiences are, as Toby Miller puts it, "the opium of television" (92). However, as most television scholars will argue, television is a hegemonic function that *becomes* our presence of mind. In other words, "TV producers want to *make audiences*, not simply *attract viewers*" (247). Jennifer L. Pozner argues that all media "shape and reflect cultural perceptions of who we are, what we're valued for, what we want, what we need, what we believe about ourselves and others—and what we should consider 'our place' in society" (21). Television, in particular, is incredibly forceful in influencing how we view ourselves and the world. While we are not all affected in the same way by any single episode of a given television show or series, "it is the aggregate of messages that enter our minds." She follows that we consume them "as automatically and unconsciously as the air we breathe" (21). Television is more than commodity, then; it is a generally passive mode of entertainment that viewers allow to shape who they are politically, sexually, morally, and culturally. Perhaps this is due to television's unique dual position as both a communal and private experience. It is "a feature of modern *public* life which has a place in nearly every *private* home" (Miller 99).

The presence of the "real" on television is not new, but the emergence of reality television has been deeply influential in the ways we experience "reality" on television. The viewer experiences sports, news programs, talk shows, special reports, reality television, and documentary as non-fiction and therefore, to some extent, true-to-life. While the viewer might acknowledge the influence of editors, directors, and even some scripting, reality television is still purportedly showing us something based in reality. Arild Fetveit, who argues that digital manipulation and image generation have caused a tension in photographic discourse that is further complicated by the advent of reality television, posits that reality television is an "effort to reclaim what seems to be lost after digitalization. [That is,] not only a belief in the evidential powers of photography but as much a sense of being in contact with the world by way of indexicality." He furthers that "The powerful urge for a sense of contact with the real is inscribed in much of the reality TV footage" (551). In other words, reality television is a reclamation of the pre-digital television era and its ability to make sense of the world through its implied "sense of connectedness" (551). Reality television allows us to attempt to reconnect with the world. More than mere voyeurism, it allows us to look at and identify with not actors, but people who are real, ordinary, and are either like us or people we know. Further, reality television also offers us a safe distance from the reality we are viewing. Because we can easily flip the channel, we find comfort in the idea that even though it looks like reality, "It is not reality, it is reality *TV*, a reality *show* (551). Television's communal privacy contributes to a new kind of freak show viewing. It provides us with the thrill and excitement of reality while offering the safety and comfort of our own homes. Therefore, it attempts to take away the cultural gap of otherness and put another one in its place: the televisual gap.

Television, and reality television in particular, seems to want to give us access to the freak show and even offer us something more than the freak show—after all, there are freak bodies all over television—but it can't seem to reach the moments it aims for. This is because when reality television does explore the freak body, it is aligned with institutions of heteronormativity—marriage, heterosexuality, domesticity—in an attempt to normalize freakishness. For example, we can look beyond the disabled bodies that star in *Little People, Big World* because they are domesticated bodies; the show's characters are married, heterosexual, and are grounded in the domestic setting of their family farm. Here, it is as if the institution of heterosexual marriage does away with or forgives some of their otherness.

I explore similar attempts at heteronormativity briefly in the heavily freak-populated lineup on the TLC network, as well as in two documentaries, *Murderball* and *Push Girls*. While I find that the singular nature of the documentary successfully finds para-freak show moments because of its engagement with realness, veil of expertise, and contact with the sexual freak body, ultimately these portrayals do not close the gap between freak and norm bodies but instead underpin notions of cultural normality.

## THE FREAK BODY ON TLC

Perhaps nowhere is the freak body more familiar on television than on the TLC network. Often referred to on internet blogs and forums as the "freak show channel," it almost solely offers reality and documentary programs that focus on physical otherness. These include domestic reality shows such as *A Baby Story* and *Four Weddings*; tattoo reality shows including *Miami Ink* and *New York Ink*; big people reality shows like *Big Love* and *600 lb Mom*; little people shows *The Little Couple*, *The Little Chocolatiers* and, one of their biggest hits, *Little People, Big World*; reality shows and mini-documentaries about sexual and reproductive freakishness including *19 Kids and Counting*, *John and Kate Plus Eight*, *Sister Wives*, *I Didn't Know I Was Pregnant*, and *Virgin Diaries*; and finally deformity documentaries such as *The Man With Half a Body*, *Bubble*

*Skin Man, My Forty Year Old Child, The Man Who Lost His Face, Born Without a Face, 16 Year Old Toddler,* and *Medical Mysteries.*

TLC's lineup of shows has obvious parallels to the traditional freak show lineup: tattooed men and women, big and little people, sexual miscreants such as hermaphrodites and bearded women, and the disabled. We still see unusual bodies at the few actual freak shows that do exist today, such as Coney Island's "Sideshow at the Seashore" which is comprised of tattooed people, bearded women, and big and little people who all perform novelty acts, so it is no surprise to see these bodies also represented on television. TLC typically represents these bodies in benign ways in its series rather than one-time documentaries, thus we are exposed to them much more often and become used to seeing their bodies. While the episodic nature of the freak show and the talk show kept its viewers entertained and surprised again and again with new freaks, the episodic nature of television does the opposite. Because we are exposed to the same bodies over an extended period of time (*Little People, Big World* aired for six full seasons over the course of four years), those bodies become benign (i.e. boring) to the viewer.

The shock factor of shows like *The Little Couple* and *Little People, Big World* is short-lived and prescriptive. The shows attempt to celebrate these families for achieving access to normal cultural institutions and rites of passage such as getting married, having babies, having successful careers, and driving cars. Because we do not see them in grotesque, sexual, or subversive ways, we are initially shocked by their relative normality, not their abnormality. In other words, the families that appear on these shows are normalized because, though their bodies are different, they are not staged in sensational ways. The only thing interesting about the show is the family's short stature and it is rarely a focal point unless the show is pursuing a supercrip plotline. Therefore, the bodies on *Little People, Big World* and others like it are not freak bodies because they are not exhibited as such. The shows are meant to familiarize and normalize and are effective in doing so to the point of becoming uninteresting.

Even TLC's series *Abby and Brittany*, a reality series about conjoined twenty-something girls (see Fig. 4.1), managed to bore and frustrate audiences, the former because nothing particularly interesting or exciting happens on the show and the latter because the questions the audience wants answered aren't. *Abby and Brittany* supposes that, like the little people shows mentioned above, audiences want to see a freakish body doing normal things. However, it seems all people want to know about

**Fig. 4.1**   Abby and Brittany Hensel, *TLC* 2012

these conjoined twins is how they have sex.[3] Since the girls share a pelvis and thus one vagina and set of reproductive organs, questions about their sex lives illicit confusion and a perverse curiosity, as in *Geek Love*. Can the two girls marry the same man or different men? If one is kissed, does the other feel it? When they have sex, do they both feel the orgasm? Who is their sexual partner actually having sex with? If the other doesn't condone it, is it rape? Is it incest? Polygamy? What about masturbation? Parenting? *Abby and Brittany* does not attempt to answer these questions but rather tries to normalize the girls' joined body.

Rather than seeing the "reality" of what it means to live as a conjoined twin and the complications and complexities involved in having such a body, the show instead tries to prove the girls' heteronormality.

---

[3] I have not been able to find a single comment-enabled article about the twins on the internet that is *not* mainly comprised of graphic questions about the girls' sex lives.

They are sorority girls, student teachers, athletes, and world-travelers. This all-American college girl image fights against the concept of freak-ishness but, like *Little People, Big World*, the end result is boredom. The only thing interesting about their lives is their body and the show is framed in such a way that suggests the viewer is supposed to look past it. However, despite the fact that we see the girls' body(ies) over the course of an entire season of episodes, it never feels normal to watch them and it doesn't seem possible to look past their difference. This suggests that despite the mode of presentation, some bodies simply cannot be normalized.

TLC gets closer to the freak show when it perpetuates paradigms such as the medical model of disability and depicts freakish bodies through the mode of documentary, distinctly different in its singular nature from television series. Two interesting examples are found in *The Man Who Lost His Face* and *The Man with the 200 LB Tumor*; both are hour long documentaries which aired on TLC in 2011 and 2012, respectively. These documentaries perpetuate harmful narratives such as that of the white expert/savior and the monstrous other while they also reinforce the medical model of disability as well as the pity paradigm, and oper-ate within conventions of melodrama. Both documentaries carry an air of impermanence and rarity; rather than the long-term exposure of *Little People, Big World*, you will only see these bodies once. This is, of course, more effective in shocking and engaging audiences.

The men in both documentaries are situated as freaks in need of repair. *The Man Who Lost His Face* documents a Portuguese man, Jose, as he travels to America to undergo the removal of a massive facial tumor that has blinded him in one eye and prevents him from being able to eat properly. "In search of a miracle," Jose and his family find a specialist in Chicago who is willing to perform the necessary surgeries to correct what the doctor calls the "hellish image" of Jose's face. A similar story, *The Man with the 200 Lb. Tumor* tells the story of Hai Win, a 31-year-old Vietnamese man who has, at most, a year to live if he doesn't have his parasitic 200-pound tumor removed. He too enlists the help of an American specialist—the same surgeon, in fact, who operates on Jose.

The shows speak to the freak show in various ways. Their format fol-lows the freak show blueprint closely: an exaggerated title to sell the show, an overdramatic hype-man/narrator to keep viewers enthralled, the freak who we can simultaneously pity, blame, relate to, and reject. Viewers are directed to regard Jose and Hai with sympathy. Jose is in pain, cannot eat or see properly, and is embarrassed to leave his home. A current-day Elephant Man, Jose is shown walking the streets of Chicago before his surgery. He is embarrassed and his family is angered when tourists stare and take pictures of him. His sister, Edith, yells at people and makes them delete the pictures, shaming them for doing exactly what viewers are doing at home: staring at a freak. Whether viewers at home are excused from feeling the same shame of the photographers is unclear. Jose and his family allowed themselves to be filmed for this television show, after all, and in doing so have given viewers permission to stare. This suggests that we can only safely stare at the freak body from a distance, where we can look but the freak cannot return our gaze.

Hai is bedridden from the gigantic tumor that has already resulted in the loss of one of his legs. Left helpless from the sheer size and weight of the tumor, Hai's family has always taken care of him. When he was young, for example, his brothers had to carry him to school because his tumor was so large that he could not walk. This information is conveyed in a way that implies Hai is parasitic to his family just as his tumor is to him. At age 17, the tumor in his right leg became so big that his leg was amputated. The tumor quickly grew back and appears so large that it actually looks like a massive, misshapen leg. The viewer certainly pities Hai, but the family is painted as being so ignorant that we are also left suspicious: could something have been done to prevent or permanently remove Hai's tumor when he was a child? This suspicion is validated when his mother says, "you are what you eat but he doesn't eat much so why does the tumor keep growing?" The viewer wants to blame Hai and his family for allowing this to happen. We wonder why he didn't seek the "real" medical opinion of an educated doctor sooner. Of course, we also feel guilty when we see that Hai lives in such a remote village that a group of men must carry him up a treacherous dirt hill in order to reach a roadway and allow him to embark on an eight hour drive to the nearest hospital. The scene underscores how Hai's journey should be portrayed as scientific, exploring the cause and removal of the tumor, but instead it is sensational, melodramatic, and suggests that other cultures, or even poverty itself, are responsible for freakishness.

To the end of portraying Jose and Hai as exotic bodies, both men are often shown and referred to as being monstrous and freakish. To situate Jose as a monstrous other, the documentary highlights him saying that he feels like a burden to his family and that he thinks his tumor is a punishment. He is humanized by the focus on his family throughout the documentary, in particular his sister, Edith. However, repeated references such as those above position Jose as a pitiable freak who has done something to deserve his fate. Opposing the view of the monstrous body, Jose's surgeon, Dr. McKinnon, even refers to the tumor as "a monster that he has lived with for many years." There is a blurring, then, between the monster and the man, ultimately positioning the man as a victim of the monster within and thus working in the mode of the melodrama.

Hai is similarly both othered and humanized. His tumor is referred to as the "monster that was killing him." Despite this monstrosity, however, Hai almost always appears smiling, showing immense bravery in the face of his disfigurement. Meant to be inspirational, Hai borders on appearing idiotic; surely, we think, if he really understood how dangerous his tumor was, he would not be so casual and happy. There is an unbelievable media presence surrounding his case; it is certainly a modern-day sideshow. People peer into his hospital room and cameras follow them around, interviewing doctors and family members. The case is such a media sensation, in fact, that Hai's surgery is broadcast live in the hospital for viewers to watch. After the operation, "news of the incredible surgery" immediately goes viral. As he recovers, reporters from around the globe gather at the hospital. That Hai is to be regarded as a sideshow spectacle is clear, in other words, because he is so blatantly treated like one.

The displaying of tortured exotic bodies is a long American tradition with roots in both the freak show and lynching photography. Like the cartes de visite, these images "provided a safe context for talking about" unusual bodies, in this case, racial bodies (Fahy 20). Fahy notes that "widespread concerns about miscegenation and passing" in the late nineteenth and early twentieth centuries were indicative of an "increasingly fluid relationship between black and white [which] exacerbated white fears about America's future." Images of African American bodies as victims were therefore important symbols for white America that reinforced their believed superiority over other races. In other words, these images were a way to keep black Americans "in their place" (20). The bodies of Jose and Hai are doubly marked freak because they are both exotic and disabled bodies. Their bodies become sites inscribed with narratives about racial superiority, monstrosity, pity, fear, and Western medical practices.

Further drawing out this narrative, the white American surgeon and hospital staff are cast as both experts and saviors to the monstrous bodies of Jose and Hai. As with the freak show, a white doctor is brought into cure and authenticate Jose and Hai's bodies and backstories. As Rachel Adams tells us: "Freak shows had always drawn on ethnographic and medical discourses to grant legitimacy to the fantastic narratives they wove around the bodies on display." Often, the expert was cast as the person who discovered and "saved" the freak from their unfortunate circumstances and brought them safely to America to be studied and, of course, displayed to the public until they could be cured. Of course, these "experts" and "saviors" benefited tremendously from their associations with the freak show. They were provided with a "reliable supply" of freakish bodies to examine, treat, and study (28).

Such experts were important in that they authenticated the freak body, but their presence also "authorize[d] one person to gaze at another" (28). Their juxtaposition next to the exotic and, in these cases, deformed foreigners, emphasizes the differences between normal and abnormal bodies. In highlighting the differences between the white doctors and the non-white patients, Jose and Hai are characterized as ignorant, helpless, and pitiable. Hai's story, in particular, really plays to this narrative. Hai's case is championed first by Amanda Schumacher, a white activist from the Tree of Life Foundation International. She brings Hai's condition to the attention of Dr. McKinnon, the only doctor willing to perform the dangerous surgery. Because Hai cannot fly, McKinnon has to convince a Vietnamese hospital to host the surgery rather than to bring him to America. Forced to operate on Hai with a Vietnamese surgical team, McKinnon yells at the nurses and other doctors, commenting on their poor communication skills throughout the 12 h long surgery. There is a clear line drawn between the white doctor and the foreign medical staff. Afterwards, he lays on compliments about what a great hospital and staff they have but his superiority is made clear to the viewer. Without the American savior, Hai would surely be dead.

Both documentaries have unexpectedly ambiguous endings. While they wrap up with narratives about the bravery and miraculous nature of the men's journeys, the men remain freaks; they are both still disabled (though their conditions have been improved) and othered. Hai's story ends with McKinnon praising Hai as an inspiration who will give people courage. At the end of the episode, despite only having one leg, Hai is able to use a walker to walk by himself for the first time in over a decade. The surgeon is the hero, and Hai is the medical miracle.

For Jose, after a 15 h long surgery, the tumor is removed and his life is no longer in danger. However, he is more horrifying to look at now than he was with the tumor. His face is misshapen and very heavily bandaged. A facial reconstruction surgery, performed eight weeks after the tumor is removed, lasts 12 h and includes the removal of more tumors, moving Jose's mouth to the center of his face, and reconstructing his nose. He is shown agitated and anxious after this last surgery, having terrible psychiatric reaction to the surgery and medications. He appears as a monster, out of control and hideous. Jose is unused to how his face feels without the tumors and the unfamiliarity upsets him greatly. Again, we see a dual persona in Jose: he is not quite the monster, but there is clearly something monstrous within his body.

The documentaries also serve as examples of how TLC has perpetuated the myth of the racial freak, once immensely popular in the freak show. As noted by Adams, confrontations between audiences and the many "savages, cannibals, and missing links that frequented the sideshow platform" were shaped in ways which "provided occasions for viewers … to consider their superiority to representatives of primitive cultures" (31). Ethnographic freaks were painted as deviant, abnormal, and either terrifyingly savage or ridiculously ignorant and harmless. The common pairing of racial freaks with animals suggests that they should be feared for both their savagery and ignorance. For example, Ota Benga, the young African who was displayed in a cage at the Bronx Zoo in 1906, had teeth that were sharpened into fangs. This served as clear evidence to audiences of his cannibalism, "a practice," Adams notes "that located him halfway between animal and human" (33).

In these two TLC specials, we see a mixture of both freak show depictions; the terrifying monstrosity is found in the disability itself while the exotic otherness of the men is rendered harmless by their ignorance and joviality. The men are particularly harmless due to the distinct absence of sexual desire like Franklin, Merrick, and the other male freak bodies I have studied. Most often paired with animals instead of women, the ethnographic freaks of the sideshow were rarely if ever sexualized. They were frightening enough, it seems, without adding the threat of sexual potency to their characterizations. We only have access to the freak body on TLC, ultimately, if the freaks themselves are perpetuating negative and stereotypical narratives about race, gender, and disability and, perhaps most importantly, if they are culturally and geographically other.

## HYPERSEXUALITY AND GENDER IN DOCUMENTARY

*Murderball* and *Push Girls,* documentaries about the lives of people with disabilities, portray disability with an edge of realness that isn't found on the TLC network. Documentary is, in fact, often categorized by its association with the real. Building on John Grierson's definition of documentary as the "creative treatment of actuality," Bill Nichols proposes more specifically that we can begin to understand the genre by categorizing documentary as film that

> ...speaks about situations and events involving real people (social actors) who present themselves to us as themselves in stories that convey a plausible proposal about, or perspective on, the lives, situations, and events portrayed. The distinct point of view of the filmmaker shapes this story into a way of seeing the historical world directly rather than into a fictional allegory. (14)

Nichols clarifies, further, that documentary is "a representation of a world we already occupy," and not a "reproduction of reality" (10). Though cumbersome, this definition captures the idea that documentaries are categorically creative endeavors that are ultimately and immovably grounded in reality. As commonly understood, documentaries are representations of events that actually transpired and are acted by the people who actually experienced those events.

Further, the concept of indexicality is important in characterizing documentary. Nichols defines indexical quality as an "uncanny sense of a document, or image that bears a strict correspondence to what it refers to" (34). The indexical quality of an image refers to,

> the way in which its appearance is shaped or determined by what it records: a photo of a boy holding his dog will exhibit, in two dimensions, an exact analogy of the spatial relationship between the boy and his dog in three dimensions; a fingerprint will show exactly the same pattern of whorls as the finger that produced it; a photocopy replicates an original precisely; markings on a fired bullet will bear an indexical relationship to the specific gun barrel through which it passed. The bullet's surface "records" the passage of that bullet through the gun barrel with a precision that allows forensic science to use it as documentary evidence in a given case. (34)

Filmic sounds and images also have an indexical nature. It is this quality, according to Nichols, that "makes the documentary image appear as a vital source of evidence about the world" (34). Thus the documentary can stand in as a form of evidence; it is perhaps as real as viewers can get to an event without actually being there.

Documentary, to a lesser extent than reality television, does suggest a specific interpretation of the people and events it portrays. Again, it is not reality, but a creative interpretation of the real. Distinguishing the documentary from other genres is the oscillation that occurs between the reality of what we view and the artistic slant that the documentary inevitably suggests. However, viewers tend to have an implicit trust in documentary which suggests that the genre's representation is weighed more heavily than any creative influence. There exists an air of exclusivity and seriousness around documentary that increases its realness. Because of its claims to truth, viewers implicitly see documentary as being authoritative, academic, and serious. Documentary is high-brow, whereas reality television is undoubtedly lowbrow. Finally, documentary does not need to concern itself with censorship and can simply show more than other forms.

While television does not give meaningful access to the freak show due to its episodic nature and attempts to normalize the freak body, the documentary is not so limited. Unlike episodic television, the documentary gives us a single viewing. While many documentaries may be longer than a single episode of a television show, we are only exposed to the images in a documentary for an hour or two as opposed to a television show that takes place over the course of one or more seasons. This means that the documentary has more opportunity to shock us with its images because we do not see them long enough to become accustomed to their differences or uniqueness. Documentary claims authenticity and expertise, like the freak show. However, its position as a high-brow genre allows it to be taken more seriously. The documentary can be more real than the freak show; it can allow us access to those behind-the-scenes moments that the freak show does not permit.

Like TLC's reality shows, the freak bodies in *Murderball* and *Push Girls* reaffirm familiar social structures such as heterosexuality, traditional gender roles, marriage, and domesticity. Unlike television series, however, they have more access to freak show moments. They gain this access from their exaggerated embodiments and representations of sex and gender. I refer to this hyperbolized depiction of sexuality and gender as hypersexual and hypergendered throughout my discussion. In using these terms, I refer to the extreme prominence, almost to the point of comedy, of embodying heterosexuality and perpetuating traditional gender roles. The characters I examine are not simply masculine and feminine; they are the embodiment of those terms to extremes.

Throughout this book, I have shown how freak bodies have been desexualized. The bodies I have explored have been sexually lacking or dysfunctional in some way (This will change in the next two chapters when I discuss disability porn and then Lady Gaga and Marilyn Manson and the ways in which they embody grotesque sexuality). Freak bodies and disabled bodies are generally not portrayed sexually. The freak body was often displayed in ways that *suggested* sexuality—a little woman was paired with a giant and their baby, for example—but their sex lives were not explicitly discussed. In the rare instances that freak sexuality was overtly displayed, such as in *Freaks*, it was quickly cast into the shadows.

For essayist Nancy Mairs, the disjunction between the disabled self and the sexual body can be blamed on the Western tradition of distinguishing the mind and soul from the body. In her essay "Carnal Acts," she notes that we have widened the rift between the "I" and the body in the ways in which we treat our bodies. For Mairs, the female body in particular is often a body of shame, "since so much of it is in fact hidden, dark, secret, carried about on the inside where, even with the aid of a speculum, one can never perceive all of it in the plain light of day, a graspable whole." Her disabled body, then, is doubly shameful, "not merely by the homo-sexual standards of patriarchal culture but by the standards of physical desirability erected for every body in our world" (Mairs 53–54).

Like Mairs, Kenny Fries is doubly othered as a gay man with "congenital deformities of the lower extremities."[4] For Fries, however, the disabled male body can still be a sexual body, though it is not a powerful one. In his poem "Beauty and Variations," for example, he questions his lover, wondering if he were to break his lover's bones and make them look like his "twisted legs" if he would still desire him or would it "disturb the balance //of [their] desire?" (2: 1–5). Later, he accuses

---

[4] Fries was born with congenital deformities of his feet and legs, specifically with three toes on each foot and undersized legs that were twisted "like pretzels" and missing bones. Fries, "Introduction" 1.

his lover of being attracted to his legs not out of sexual attraction but something "beyond desire" (4: 4–5). Finally, Fries, like Mairs, becomes separated from his body when he asks, "What does my body want from yours?" (5:7). As in another of his poems, "Excavation," his sexuality is resolutely tied to the same body that has been called "*Freak, midget, three-toed /bastard*" (7). This poem, like "Beauty and Variations," questions how such a body can be a powerful, sexual one.

People with disabilities have historically been excluded from sexual culture and are only very recently becoming visible as sexual beings. As Tobin Siebers so plainly puts it, "disabled people experience sexual repression, possess little or no sexual autonomy, and tolerate institutional and legal restrictions on their intimate conduct" (*Disability Theory* 136). The disabled population has long been plagued with the myth that they do not have or desire sexual identities. The stigma that physical impairment implies sexual dysfunction or absence is clearly harmful to a person's identity but seems even more compacted for men who often associate their perceived loss of sexual identity as a loss of masculinity.

Disability literature has not, however, changed the cultural stereotypes that see sex and disability as each an "occasion for marginalization or marveling" (McRuer and Mollow 1). The reason for this is quite simple: outside of classrooms, no one is reading it. The disability documentary has more opportunity to break cultural stereotypes about people with disabilities. The documentary *Murderball* and the television docuseries *Push Girls*, although similar in medium to the reality television shows I've discussed, stand apart in various ways, most notably in that both are intended for more high-brow audiences. The simple absence of the label "reality tv" separates them as being intended for more serious audiences, while the distribution of each of them, the former as an independent film documentary and the latter as a docuseries on the independent *Sundance* channel, gives them an air of exclusivity that sets them apart from popular culture. *Murderball* was produced by MTV Films and was nominated for an Academy Award. While this suggests mainstream success, the film only showed in limited theaters for three months and was considered a box-office failure despite universally positive critical reviews. Both titles have had some mainstream success but still remain on the margin of pop culture.

I have chosen these two specific documentaries because of the ways in which (hetero) sexuality is not merely acknowledged in them but is brought to center stage. Both documentaries vehemently reject Mairs'

**Fig. 4.2**    Mark Zupan in the opening scene of *Murderball* (Rubin and Shapiro 2005)

shame and Fries' doubt. For the men and women in these documentaries, being disabled does not mean being absent from sexuality. In fact, gender and sexuality almost always seem to be at the forefront of the individual personalities being documented. While this often results in hypergendered and clichéd characterizations, *Murderball* and *Push Girls* normalize the sexually active disabled body through their contact with cultural yardsticks of normality.

## *Murderball*

*Murderball* is a 2005 documentary that follows the rivalry between the US and Canadian men's wheelchair rugby teams as they prepare for and participate in the 2004 Paralympics. Wheelchair rugby, originally called murderball, is played in "gladiator, battling machine, Mad Max style wheelchairs" (Barounis 58) that can withstand being rammed into one another over and over again. The documentary's opening scene is of Mark Zupan, the film's central focus, as he removes his jeans and puts on a pair of basketball shorts. Zupan himself appears fragile and awkward, as he shuffles around in his chair to first lower his jeans, and then lifts each leg separately out of the pants. His arduous movements contrast the bold tribal tattoo that takes up much of his left calf. His bedroom is both sad and powerful; it is dreary and unkempt, though the unmade bed, empty beer bottles, and studded belt on the floor add a masculine edge to the décor. Zupan removes his shirt to reveal a muscular upper body and more tattoos, and rolls awkwardly out of the frame (see Fig. 4.2).

This introductory scene is representative of the entire documentary; it is a visual mash-up between what the viewer expects to see—a weakened man who is dependent on others—and the actual reality—strong, independent, and rugged—of the life and body of the disabled man being filmed. Cynthia Barounis reflects on the opening scene as well, noting that:

> The moment that the camera zooms in on Zupan's tattoo is the moment that the man becomes more than mere flesh. And it is precisely at that point that the intimacy and vulnerability of the scene's opening is eclipsed by a prosthetic remaking of the body – an elaborate new technology of gender. We hear and see the rip of duct tape, the whirring of the wheel, and the clanging of metal. Later, we will watch an animated clip in which metal screws are incorporated into the skeletal drawing of a spine; the image gradually fades into a shot of the actual scars that mark one player's neck. (58–59)

Just as new bodies are built, so are new concepts of masculinity. Zupan's tattoo marks the body *as* a marked body. In other words, it signals to the viewer that the body has been modified and when the scene is paired with images of metal being inserted into both a chair and a body, the documentary asks us to see the disabled body in a new way. The disabled man is, in this case, modified—made a warrior—through its fusion with metal and technology. As Barounis continues, "If, according to the logic of the film, it was the amplification of ordinary masculinity that led to Zupan's injury, then this extraordinarily refashioned machinic masculinity is nothing less than mythic" (59).[5]

---

[5] The "the amplification of ordinary masculinity" that Barounis is referring to is how Zupan was injured. He passed out drunk in the back of a friend's pick-up truck and his friend, also drunk, drove home without knowing that Zupan was in the truck's bed. He crashed into a ditch, throwing Zupan's body down the side of the ditch where he hung on to a branch for hours until he was found.

Many have applauded *Murderball* for its portrayal of men with disabilities because the film's athletes are humanized and made relatable in their portrayals.[6] They are portrayed in such a way that we are able to sympathize with them without having to pity them. Others have slammed the documentary, arguing that it only shatters stereotypes about disability through reinforcing patriarchal, misogynistic, and heteronormative views of gender and sexuality.[7]

Zupan and the documentary's other male characters perpetuate these negative cultural perceptions in order to reassert an assumed loss of male power. Barounis has argued that the popularity of the documentary is ultimately a success for disability activism not despite but in part because "its most radical features are simultaneously its most conventional." The film succeeds in avoiding traditional disability clichés, argues Barounis, especially the belief that the disabled body is a fragile, non-sexual body. In order to accomplish this, the documentary reinforces what Barounis calls the "ironclad endurance of male heterosexual privilege (57). Throughout much of the documentary, it is the (unfortunately) realistic portrayal of young men as sexist fratboys that serves to humanize them and normalize their disabilities. This suggests that viewers can only overlook a social stigma such as disability as long as other norm-enforcing binaries are overtly present. (We will later see that this is true of *Push Girls*, as well.)

Barounis misses the point, however, that it is their hypermasculinity that covers up an insecure sense of sexual identity. The insecure sexual identity that often comes with being newly disabled is explored in *Murderball*. One scene in particular is rather telling. A few of the players talk about how whenever they meet women, they know that the women are wondering whether or not the men are physically capable of having sex. The film quickly flips to such an interaction and we watch one of the players, Hogsett, as he talks to a young woman. She asks him how he was injured and how his disability affects various parts of his body. Quickly, she asks the question Hogsett has been waiting for: "Is it... dead?" referring, clearly, to his penis. As he reassures her that he is fully sexually functional, the young woman breathes a sigh of relief. While the

---

[6] In fact, *most* have applauded the film as most people typically laud anything having to do with the representation of disability.

[7] Most notably, Kurt Lindemann in *Disability Studies Quarterly*.

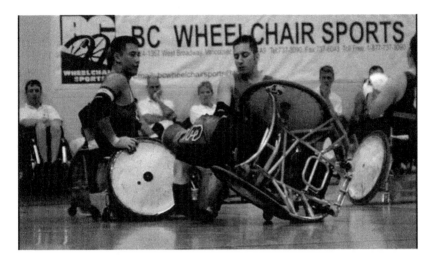

**Fig. 4.3**  Zupan gets knocked over during a game in *Murderball* (Rubin and Shapiro 2005)

exchange is uncomfortably awkward, it is interesting and unique to see the functioning of a disabled male's genitals discussed so openly, especially since, as we have seen in the cases of Franklin and Merrick, this is a topic that is often skirted around and suggested rather than openly discussed.

While the men in the film often make light of the myth that casts them as sexually disabled, it is clearly an important part of their post-disability identities. One player expresses his concern that "Women are not threatened by the guy that's in a chair [so that when] they come up, strike up great casual conversation, ... you're like, 'Okay. Is she seeing the chair or is she seeing me?'" Hogsett, on the other hand, expresses contradictory feelings about it. At one point he expresses vulnerability when he tells the girl from the above anecdote that the first time he got an erection after his disabling accident, his rehab nurse was so excited that she went and got his mother to show her Hogsett's erect penis. This embarrassing story, in which Hogsett is reduced to a child in front of his nurse and mother, is quickly dismissed when he says, "Fuck it. The more pitiful I am, the more women like me." His willingness to exploit his disability in order for the chance to sleep with women casts him as a manipulative predator rather than a helpless boy. As this illustrates, while the insecure sexual identity that often comes along with disability is explored in *Murderball*, it is quickly brushed under the rug to focus instead on the men's sexual potency. The documentary claims that it wants the men to be seen as people, flaws and all but ultimately achieves these ends by focusing on the men's misogyny and sexism as a way to excuse or overlook their disabilities.

The violent nature of wheelchair rugby allows the players a way of refusing the limitations placed on them by an ableist society (see Fig. 4.3). As Lindemann and Cherney note in "Communicating In and Through 'Murderball,'" the very act of playing wheelchair rugby is a "communicative act challenging ableist views of disability" and that "the behavior of wheelchair rugby players transforms the stigma associated with their condition via enactments of hypermasculinity" (107). The sport itself is incredibly important in the characterizations of its players as powerful and masculine bodies. Because wheelchair rugby is by its very nature such a violent sport, and because disability is a prerequisite to playing the game, the players appear hypermasculine because of their disabilities rather than in spite of them. In wheelchair rugby, disability is a "weapon to be wielded *against* one's foe." Men are not fighting against their illnesses or disabilities, but rather have "acquir[ed] an injury that enabled them to fight" (Barounis 58).

Many of the men in the documentary were injured while doing things considered masculine. It is no coincidence that the two most traditionally attractive and toughest looking men in the film were injured in the most "rugged" ways, while many of the other men who are less attractive (i.e. more deformed) were disabled through illness, a passive rather than active means of becoming disabled. The quadruple amputee, Bob Lujano, for example, lost his limbs as a result of a rare blood disease called Meningococcemia, which is a rare form of meningitis, when he was a child. On the other hand, Hogsett's spinal cord was snapped in a fist fight, while Zupan was thrown from the back of a friend's truck after he passed out drunk in the bed of it. This toughness translates awkwardly to the men's post-disability bodies. The hypermasculinity they exude would often seem crude coming from able-bodied men but is somehow made acceptable and reassuring coming from men with disabilities. That is, viewers' fears and anxieties about disabled male bodies are lessened because their bad heteronormative behavior assures the viewer that they are still looking at a normal, masculine, male body. The men's need to be hypergendered and hypersexual is a successful attempt to normalize, or to de-freak, their bodies.

One way in which the men are portrayed as hypergendered is by their need to participate in needlessly dangerous behaviors. Murderball itself is a violent and dangerous sport, but the refusal by the men to wear helmets and pads while playing is simply, as Zupan says, "a macho man thing." Another player reflects on the decision to not wear a helmet saying, "that has to go back to, you know, you don't want to look more retarded, I guess, than what we feel like we already are, you know what I mean? If you start putting a bunch of helmets on dudes in wheelchairs, there's, you know, that hurts the egos" (Lindemann and Cherney 114). For men who have already been emasculated by their chairs, wearing a helmet would take away their already frail sense of masculinity. Similarly, dangerous behaviors such as when Bob Lajuno drives without using a seatbelt or his prosthetic arms, or when Zupan goes down a moving escalator in his chair, seem pointless. Bob's prosthetics are designed to enable him to perform daily activities such as driving, and Zupan could easily take an elevator. The men's refusal to do things in the expected way seems to be a refusal to be typecast as "crippled" men.

Another way in which the men of *Murderball* refuse to be defined by their disabilities is by constantly talking about sex in aggressive ways. As Barounis notes, "When they're not giving (or getting) a beating on the court, they're drinking and having sex with women, or bragging about drinking and having sex with women" (56). The film is at its most transgressive in these scenes which is oddly a feature of the film that has received "widespread praise from its [presumably both male and female] viewers" (56). I call this odd not simply because we are culturally sheltered from the idea of a person with disabilities being sexual, but also because these scenes are often rather crude.

For example, much of this talk revolves around the fact that, as Zupan unabashedly tells us, "When you're in a chair you usually like to eat pussy." His comment is "embedded within a sentence that begins with Zupan gesturing downwards and reassuring the viewer, 'that still works'" (59). Like Hogsett's earlier conversation about the functionality of his penis, Zupan's statement seems to be both a reassurance to himself and the viewer that he is still, in fact, a man. By stating that he likes to eat pussy even though he can maintain an erection, Zupan hypersexualizes himself, ultimately claiming that just because he can use his penis doesn't mean that it's the only thing that makes him a viable sexual partner.

A later conversation in which the guys make fun of a fellow player for not "liking big tits" reflects this. Though the men tease him, the player insists that it makes him more of a man for knowing what turns him on and not just going for what the other men find sexually attractive.

The cunnilingus narrative among disabled male athletes is, surprisingly, a popular one. Lindemann and Cherney recount, for example, a conversation among some players at a regional rugby tournament about one of the players, a quadruple amputee, eating a hamburger:

> Turning to Steve and Meagan, Doug laughs, "Did you see the freak show? Boomer was trying to eat a burger." Doug mimes the action, using his elbows as if they were the stumps of Boomer's amputated arms, awkwardly grabbing an imaginary hamburger and eating it. Meagan, Steve's able-bodied girlfriend, asks him incredulously, "Well, Doug. How else is he supposed to eat it? His arms and legs are gone." Perhaps this is the line he's been waiting for, because Doug, smiling broadly, responds, "Chow down, you know." He pauses for effect and then continues, "Chow down like he's chowing on something else." Doug bends his neck, positioning his head close to the imaginary plate in front of him, and opens and closes his mouth, flicking his tongue with great gusto. It's obvious that he's miming the act of cunnilingus. (119)

In this example, Doug essentially claims that "eating pussy" acts as a replacement for something Boomer cannot do properly: eat food. Or, in other words, that the thing he cannot do—eat food—should be overlooked for what he can do—eat pussy—and thus Boomer is not emasculated but sexualized. Lindemann and Cherney add that "[i]ronically, the assertion of traditional masculine norms is made possible through an acknowledgment of the lack of traditionally masculine characteristics, like possessing a strong, able body" (119). Lindemann and Cherney refer to this as ironic masculinity: "ironic because the assertion of traditional, able-bodied masculinity comes by way of highlighting through talk a player's 'lack' of characteristics of traditional masculinity" (118). In other words, he's made a man by acknowledging non-masculine characteristics and reasserting hetero-masculine ones: by focusing on his ability to eat pussy, Boomer's body does not have to be strong or able-bodied. The other players want to show how he is heterosexually successful rather than where his body fails him.

The rugby culture allows men with disabilities to reconnect with parts of their identities that many feared would be lost after their disabilities. By emulating ableist norms—"macho posturing about athletic ability and jibes about sex and sexual orientation" (118)—the men regain access to their sexual identities, albeit through reinstating misogynistic norms. The film is quite vocal about the ways in which rugby does not rehabilitate one's body but one's lifestyle and sense of self. As one player in *Murderball* notes, "Everybody who is with us now are in their first or second year. Their rugby skills are getting better, which is great. Before it's over, you know, they're driving, they're no longer living at their parents' house, and they've got a girlfriend now." It is through the exaggerated imitation of heteronormative masculinity that these men are able to shed some of the stigma that tells them that they are not real men as long as they use a chair.

Early in the documentary Zupan tells the cameras that when other men "talk shit" to him about being in a wheelchair he encourages physical encounters. "Come on, hit me," he'll taunt them and when they don't, he says, he notes the irony in his willingness to fight able-bodied men and their refusal to "hit a kid in a chair." Zupan's point is the subtext of the entire documentary: the men of *Murderball* often come across as misogynistic, self-absorbed assholes, and that's part of the point. You shouldn't not hit Zupan because he's in a chair for the same reason that we shouldn't deny that the men in the film are often idiotic, sexist pigs. The film urges us to forget the chairs and instead to treat these men like we would an able-bodied person: hit the guy because he's an asshole and call these men out for being misogynists.

Women, both disabled and able-bodied, are noticeably marginalized in *Murderball*. Able-bodied nurses, mothers, and girlfriends dominate the female population of the film, "humaniz[ing] the disabled [male] players by occupying their traditional role[s] ... and reinforce[ing] the heterosexual masculinity of the players" (Barounis 61). Nurses and mothers in the film reinforce traditional female gender roles in their positions as caregivers, while the able-bodied, heterosexual, and sexually active girlfriends in the documentary serve as a reminder that the men are indeed heterosexually potent. While these women help to characterize the men in the film, their presence also reminds us that there is no "viable space" for the disabled female athlete; her presence is not only unnecessary but "becomes a palpable threat to the narrative glue that holds masculinity, disability, and heteronormativity firmly together" (61).

The few disabled women athletes who do appear in *Murderball* are visibly different from the male athletes. As Barounis points out, in a brief glimpse of the female volleyball team, all of whom have had leg amputations, the women appear low to the ground and do not use any prosthetics, wheelchairs, or equipment (62). This sharply contrasts the male images in the film which never show the men without some sort of modern aid. Whether it be a brace, prosthetic, or wheelchair, the men have medically modified bodies. Like Marilyn Manson's use of modern medical equipment which we will see in the final chapter, the men in the film signify a new freak show, while the women in *Murderball*, because they appear in their naturally disabled form (without medical aids) are barbaric throwbacks to the old freak show and are thus more startling to us than, for example, men discussing crude sexual behavior.

Female athletes with disabilities are not just absent from this particular documentary; in general, disabled female bodies are "not celebrated as having been liberated from oppressive conventions of gender," nor are they ever the objects of Laura Mulvey's heterosexual male gaze, and they are never the victims of Garland-Thomson's "the stare" (Barounis 61). In short, they are highly invisible in all contexts, but are especially absent as objects of athletic ability or sexual desire. *Push Girls* seeks to correct both of these cultural oversights by positioning its cast of disabled women as highly physical and athletic, as well as hypersexualized and feminine.

### *Push Girls*

*Push Girls* occupies an in-between space in my discussion. Though it is a reality television series, it has certain characteristics that make it feel more like a documentary. Part of this stems from its home on the Sundance Channel, a network that is tied to the Sundance Institute and the Sundance Film Festival, both of which are highly esteemed in the film industry. The network advertises showing, "credible, authentic, and emotionally immersive stories of Invention, Fashion, Film, Travel, Design, and Enterprise" (*Sundance Channel*). It mostly airs independent films and documentaries as well as some original series. In reviews and articles, *Push Girls* seems never to be referred to as a reality show, but instead as "original nonfiction," "docuseries," or "docudrama," and is described as being "as real as it gets," "realer than real," and "non-sensational."[8] In the press release announcing the introduction of the show to Sundance's lineup, it is referred to as a docuseries, not a reality show and, interestingly, parallels itself with *Murderball*. The press release reads:

> In the same way "Murderball," winner of the 2005 Audience Award for Best Documentary at the Sundance Film Festival, took the lid off the competitive world of "wheelchair rugby," Sundance Channel is bringing an unfettered, uncensored glimpse at what it means to be sexy, ambitious and living with paralysis in Hollywood with "Push Girls", a new original nonfiction series. ("Sundance Channel Greenlights...")

The alignment with documentary in both language and form, and the subsequent move away from reality television, suggests that the show wants to be taken seriously and believes itself to be showing a true-to-life, unfettered representation of the lives of the women in the show.

The premiere episode introduces the show's subjects—Tiphany, Angela, Mia, and Auti—who use wheelchairs in their daily lives. All four women are thin, attractive, and exude happiness. They are shown living lives that are in some ways more interesting than the average woman's. We watch them as they work out, dance at clubs, experiment with their sexuality, apply for modeling jobs, enter able-bodied dance competitions, and drive expensive sports cars. They'd be real-life Barbie dolls if they could walk.

Echoing Zupan's *Murderball* narrative is Tiphany Adams, an attractive blonde who tells her "miraculous" story to viewers while driving fast in a Mustang. Tiphany was in a car accident in which she was hit head-on at 135 miles per hour. Pronounced dead at the scene, Tiphany "fought for [her] life" and survived. We quickly find out that Tiphany, who clearly likes tight, revealing clothes and stiletto heels, loves to flirt and "yes, [she] can have sex. Lots and lots of sex." She believes that most people "haven't seen sexy in a wheelchair" and that's why they "can't fathom it." Future episodes highlight a bisexual relationship that Tiphany is currently "experimenting with."

Her roommate is Angela Rockwood, a former lingerie model, who had a "practically perfect" life before a car accident caused her severe

---

[8] See McNamara, Oates, Pfefferman, and Zimmerman and Cooper.

spinal cord injuries. Angela is now a quadriplegic; the other girls are all paraplegic, meaning they are only paralyzed from the waist down, while Angela has little movement in her upper body and none below her waist. We learn that she is separated from the former *21 Jumpstreet* actor Dustin Nguyen, and that she is still pursuing modeling as a means to support herself.

Next is Auti Angel, a professional hip hop dancer who "grew up in the hood." At 22 years old, she "hit rock bottom" by prostituting herself to a male friend for $500. In a narrative that perpetuates the connection between morality and disability, immediately after prostituting herself she was in a car accident that "snapped [her] back in half, completing separating [her] spinal cord." Her story reads as one of moral punishment—girl sells her body, girl learns to respect and appreciate her body through its loss. Now twenty years after her accident, Auti is a self-proclaimed diva who still dances, wants to start a family with her husband, and is "more determined than ever before."

Mia, perhaps the most complex and interesting woman in the docu-series, expresses contradictory thoughts about her life and disability. On the one hand, she says that when she became paralyzed from the waist down, the result of a ruptured blood vessel in her spinal cord, she felt as though her "body had betrayed [her]," but on the other hand, she thinks she is more accepting of her disability because it was caused internally, rather than as the result of a car accident like the other three women on the show. Though we only see her smiling, she tells us that she cried for weeks on end after her paralysis but eventually got over it, completely shutting herself off emotionally. She is at a point in her life where she is struggling with whether or not to stay in a long-term relationship with her boyfriend, Dave, knowing that she wants children and he does not. She says the uncomfortable truth, that people think she should "just settle" and forego her dreams because he accepts her in her chair and most men would not.

While *Murderball* focused on promoting narratives that reinforced a patriarchal heteronormativity, *Push Girls* promotes narratives that exaggerate traditional female gender roles through the hypergendering of the women. Like *Murderball*, *Push Girls* shows how people with disabilities often perpetuate exaggerated gender narratives in order to take back some of the control they feel has been lost through their disabilities. And, like *Murderball*, *Push Girls* uses conventions of heteronormative sexuality and gender in order to attempt to normalize the disabled body.

Perhaps most shocking to viewers is the women's physical appearances. All of the girls are thin and toned, are good looking, and are fashionably dressed and made up in rather feminine outfits. Stylish boots and high heels adorn their feet, while skinny jeans and low-cut tops are their wardrobe staples. The women only appear without makeup and cute outfits when they are performing athletic activities (these include swimming, skiing, kayaking, and dancing) and even then they seem conscious of their bodies' appearances. In these situations, we often hear them muttering things about how they hate not looking cute. Tiphany in particular seems preoccupied with her looks. A gorgeous, bubbly, blonde, she is the self-proclaimed flirt of the group. Constantly talking about sex and men (and, at times, women), Tiphany seems the most aware of the importance of maintaining a feminine and sexual identity. When they take Chelsie, a newly disabled teenager, into their group, one of the first things Tiphany does is take her for her first pair of post-disability high heels. While it comes off as a somewhat shallow way to regain a sense of identity, Tiphany stresses the importance of such a small thing as shoes because she is aware of the damaging perception of women with disabilities as non-sexual and non-feminine.

The girls' interests and careers are stereotypically feminine in nature, although there is almost always a hard-edged realism that goes along with it. Angela, for example, was a model and an aspiring actress before her accident and is attempting a return to the industry as a disabled model. She admits that because she is mostly paralyzed from the neck down that she can't perform many tasks and thus couldn't do many jobs. Like the rugby players' pussy eating conversation, here Angela displays an ironic femininity. Like Boomer's ironic masculinity—replacing what he cannot do with something sexual that he can do—Angela's disabled body, which limits her ability to provide a living for herself, is the only thing that she can use to make money.

The feminizing of her body as a means of supporting herself is ironic because, like Boomer, Angela takes advantage of the ways in which her body can be successful and thus renders her disabled body moot. When Angela goes to a photographer for new modeling shots, he seems to think it's ridiculous that she wants her chair shown in the photos and thinks it's a stretch for her to model at all. Comparing her to the "the guy that didn't have the arms that wanted to pitch in baseball,"[9] he thinks she has a "very uphill battle" in returning to her former career. Determined to overcome the odds and accomplish what seems impossible, Angela refuses to accept that there may not be any modeling jobs for a woman in a wheelchair no matter how beautiful she is. Although she takes photos both with and without her chair for her portfolio, when she gets a professional modeling job, she is taken out of her chair and placed in such ways that you would not know she was disabled. Thus she is removed from the stigma of disability and is unable to show her disabled body if she wants to achieve success.

Auti's experiences as a dancer have some similar complexities. Unlike Angela, she has had a lot of success in adapting her pre-disability career as a hip hop performer to her post-disability life. Her wheelchair dance group, Colors in Motion, seems to be quite successful. Unlike Angela, whose frailer appearance is what most people would expect a disabled body to look like, Auti's body seems strong and hard, in large part because of her career in dancing. Her attitude is often just as tough such as when she tells us that even though she is used to being in her chair for the past twenty years, there are still times when she just wants to get up.

We follow her as she trains and competes in an able-bodied dance competition. She says that she does not expect the judges to take it easy on her, she wishes she could compete the way the other women in the competition can, and she feels overwhelmed by her choice to dance in the show. The honesty that she displays throughout the episode is important in that it confronts what many people are thinking as well as acknowledges the realities of her position as an outsider in the competition. When she and her partner win first place, it is an odd moment because the viewer cannot help but wonder if she really was the best dancer or if she won because of her disability. She feels that she competed and won "as a dancer and not a woman in a wheelchair" but we are left wondering if she, like Angela, can truly be separated from her chair.

Among its gendered storylines is a strong focus on the girls' sexuality and dating. Through its emphasis on physical attractiveness, dating, marriage, and having children, the show reinforces traditional,

---

[9] I can only assume that he is referring to Jim Abbott, the former MLB pitcher who was born without a right hand.

heterosexual gender narratives. Like in *Murderball*, this suggests that a realistic portrayal of women, disabled or able-bodied, would include such stereotypically gendered storylines. In the first few episodes alone, we are bombarded with messages of domesticity. Mia dumps her boyfriend because he doesn't want children. Auti wants to get pregnant but is struggling because of her disability and because of her age; at 42 and faced with medical complications, she may be unable to have a baby. Tiphany seems to be desperately trying to find someone who wants to sleep with her—man or woman. Angela, on the other hand, is left struggling and unable to care for herself physically and financially after her marriage ends. These storylines send the mixed message that although the women claim independence and do not let their disabilities stop them from living full lives, they would all be happier with a spouse and children in their lives.

However, the show also highlights how uncomfortable people are in regards to disability and sex and brings up many issues that the average viewer would not be aware of. We are also asked to watch situations and wonder what we would do in similar circumstances. For instance, in the episode "How'd I Get Here?" Tiphany and Mia go speed dating and are the only two non-able-bodied people there. The girls have normal interactions with the men and even a few phone numbers are exchanged. A seemingly normal and boring scene becomes startling when the girls point out that not a single guy asked either of them about their wheelchairs. It was clear that the men saw the wheelchairs—how could they not?—but not a single one mentioned it. Rather than a scene of social progress, the scene becomes one of awkward realization: not a single man in the room knew what to say to address the fact that the girls used wheelchairs.

The episode "Freaky Deaky" is similarly eye-opening in its comments on dating. Tiphany relates a scary story about being tipped out of her chair by a man she met online, underscoring the vulnerability wheelchair users experience in intimate relationships. However, despite this incident, she is trying to meet someone on an online dating site. She says she has no problem getting attention from men and that she thinks men often wonder what it would be like to date a girl in a wheelchair. She does, however, admit that a lot of the attention she receives is not positive; she tells us that random men tend to come up with her and tell her how gorgeous she is but that they do it in a way that suggests that they think that she is never complimented. In other words, the men pity her and try to "boost her spirits" by telling her that she's pretty because they assume no one ever says such things to her because of her chair.

Mia observes, "People have this notion that the wheelchair is a deterrent for dating or marriage. You know, they think you're being way too picky if it's a nice guy [that you break up with]. They just want you to realize that you're lucky to have any guy." Mia, like the other girls, does not tend to date disabled men, and so when she ends a relationship with a guy people are shocked and imply that she might not have another chance. However, Mia insists that even though "people assume that if you're in a wheelchair, you're going to settle for any guy's attention" that she refuses to "just settle for any guy." Though they've all had different experiences when it comes to men, Mia seems to be the most realistic and have the highest standards.

Auti, on the other hand, is the most untrusting of men and is more cautious about the idea of dating than the other girls are, which is interesting since she is the only one who is married. In this same episode, she recounts a story about the way a man spoke to her at the beach: "I remember one day I was on the beach. I had a bathing suit on and this guy comes up to me. He's like, 'You're so beautiful, it's too bad ... you can't have sex but I bet you give great head.' Who says that?" The assumption that women with disabilities cannot have sex is obviously at play here, but it is also interesting that, in this man's eyes, Auti is still clearly useful as a sexual body. This misogynistic incident immediately brings to mind the discussion about Boomer eating the hamburger. Like Boomer, Auti has physical limitations but is still objectified based on what the man assumes she can do to make up for what he perceives is a lack: give great head.

The most interesting dating experience on the show is Angela's relationship with Cody, an able-bodied guy who is twelve years her junior. The two have an interesting relationship that both Angela's friends and the viewer want to mistrust. As Auti reminds us, there are men called "wheelchasers" who fetishize women in wheelchairs.[10] Cody, however, seems to really care about Angela as he proves when he accompanies the girls on their skiing trip in order to take care of Angela, who, as a

---

[10] In a related moment, Angela teases Cody for being a "freak" because he's dating a girl in a chair. It is an odd reversal of the term. Angela may be a freak because of her quadriplegia, but Cody is a bigger freak for wanting to fuck her.

quadriplegic, needs a higher level of care than the other girls. The season finale continues to explore their relationship, particularly the fine line between being a caretaker and a lover. The girls note that Cody must "man up" to take care of Angela because of her high level of care; she needs help getting in and out of her chair, getting dressed, and inserting and removing her catheter, for example. Cody does express feeling as though he has "become a man" since dating her. The scenes in which the two navigate these parts of their relationship seem more real than other intimate moments on the show. When Mia swims for the first time since becoming disabled, for example, the viewer might feel pandered to; we know we are expected to cheer her on for overcoming an obstacle and it feels, somehow, like it could be an inauthentic moment. When Cody has to change Angela's catheter, on the other hand, the viewer knows not to cheer or feel sentimental, but is left not quite knowing what to think. It is an experience that is out of most people's frame of reference. This moment becomes an almost grotesque version of the norming reinforcements (marriage, domesticity, childbearing, etc.) that characterize the show. Cody only becomes a man through the extreme gendering and near infantalization of Angela, not through any of his own doing, and Angela becomes more stereotypically weak and female because the things she lacks are highlighted.

This is not a freak show moment, of course, because the freak show did not offer a real-life depiction of freakish bodies; audiences had no idea what their lives were like beyond the freak show stage. As a space that was solely concerned with Barnumesque hype and financial profit, the freak show did, however, commonly flirt with suggestions of what real life was like for freaks. This was done in an effort to encourage both conflict and curiosity between different bodies. However, it kept the juiciest details closeted in order to keep viewers interested. Audiences were not burdened with knowledge of the medical treatments that some of its exhibits needed to care for their disabilities, for example. And although such topics were certainly suggested through staging and narratives, audiences were not aware of the mechanics of the freaks' sexual lives.

Despite its reputation as a place of spectacle, with its "[s]weltering heat, the smells of popcorn and animal dung, abusive exchange between carnies, freaks and customers" (Adams 12), the freak show was, at its core, a place of purposeful restraint. And although most claim, as Adams does, that "the freak show paraded the deviant body for all to see" (15) in actuality, compared to modern-day reality television, the freak show hardly showed us anything *real* about the freak body at all. As many side-show performers have themselves noted, the freak show could be a very lonely place because they were hidden away from view. The fear was that people might steal them or that if audiences could see them all the time, they wouldn't pay to see them at the freak show (*Sideshow: Alive on the Inside*). When they were on stage, we saw as little as possible of their bodies; though they were spectacles, they were still subject to the decorum of the time. Exhibits were fully clothed, rarely scantily clad, and certainly never nude. Their sex lives were suggested by staging, such as the pairing and exhibiting of a giant with a midget and their child, but were never outright discussed.

The frank discussions of Angela's sex life with Cody and the necessity of him changing her catheter go way beyond anything the freak show ever revealed. *Murderball* similarly crosses boundaries of decency that the spectacular freak show only ever toed. It is in crossing these lines and overexposing the freak body that *Murderball* and *Push Girls* attempt to normalize rather than exploit the bodies they exhibit. While disabled bodies on display will always be freak bodies, the true-life portrayals shown in these two documentaries tear down the freak show's veil and confront the many taboo subjects that surround the freak body. They do this, of course, while reinforcing other markers of cultural belonging. Thus they take one step forward in their portrayal of disability and two steps back with their perpetuations of stereotypical gender and sexuality.

A fine example of this comes from Mia's swimming storyline. A former competitive swimmer, Mia has not swum since becoming disabled. Afraid of failing at an activity she loved as an able-bodied person, Mia is emotionally exposed, and also physically bare in her bathing suit, with her hair wet, and without makeup. Her body, which we see more of than we do any of the other girls, is on full display. Her lower body is clearly smaller and weaker than her strong upper body. We watch her thin, awkward legs as they trail behind her underneath the water. Her legs are unusual looking, but are not so deformed as to be considered grotesque. The access to Mia's body and emotions given to the viewer during this scene is fairly remarkable not simply because it allows the viewer such closeness to the disabled body, but because it allows the viewer access to a disabled body in a state of relative weakness. The scene suggests that we can overlook her disability but only because she appears in such a feminine state: disabled female body exposed, fragile.

Another common freak show narrative which *Push Girls* confronts is the paradigm of the inspirational disabled person. Chelsie especially fights against the need of others' to see her as an inspiration. Although the show paints Chelsie's rebellion against this role as immature, blaming it on the newness of her disability, her words still have a strong impact:

Yeah, maybe I can inspire [other people] but what does that do for me physically? All I want is to walk again ... I understand that, like, we all have our different beliefs and we all think that, yeah, this might have happened to us for a reason. Maybe it did save us. Maybe it did save me. I just don't think it's fair. I don't think it's fair that I have to suffer and try to inspire all these people to do things when I'm not getting benefitted at all, you know? Like, no one's helping me. I've helped so many people, you've helped so many people, but who's helped us, you know?

Her comment is ripe with anger which the other girls are quick to justify, noting that they felt similarly at first, but have since let go of such feelings. A later episode focuses on this same anger, showing Chelsie as she gives motivational talks at high schools. She is quick to note that she is doing it because it makes her father happy and proud, not because it's something she feels driven to do. She says that she always "puts on a happy face because no one wants to be around someone who's depressed." She feels pressure to be perfect and not make any mistakes, as if her disability is all the "fault" she can bear. Her dad feels like being a motivational speaker is her new path in life, but she clearly resents the pressure put upon her to motivate others. The show allows Chelsie to voice a significant criticism of a paradigm that casts people with disabilities as mere tools for inspiring others, what is called inspiration porn. However, as soon as she does so she is silenced by the other women. Then, the show reinforces female submission to patriarchal authority—her dad wants her be the "inspirational disabled person" and she does it despite her anger. So even when the show appears to be undoing negative perpetuations of disability, it ultimately only does so by reinforcing female subjugation.

The more "real" access we get to the girls, the more we see this archetype cement itself as a permanent and perhaps necessary cultural force. The other girls seem clear on the fact that most people will only put up with disabled people who are happy and inspiring. Though Mia claims that she never feels put upon to play the role of the "inspirational disabled person" (Schaikewitz), her and the other girls' posts on their Twitter accounts suggest otherwise. Appearing to be behind-the-scenes personal accounts, the girls often post private pictures and other intimate details of their lives. Notably, most of their posts are inspirational in nature. From Tiphany's updates about her gym routine—"I choose to take on my own challenges...DAILY!" (Adams)—to Auti's assuring a fan, "you're beautiful just the way you are!" the girls rarely post complaints and often write about beauty, self-esteem, and other "feminine" topics.

Ultimately, *Push Girls*, like *Murderball* and many other freak shows on TLC, suggests that being a freak is only okay if other cultural markers of normality are clearly present. The women on *Push Girls* get away with being disabled because they are overtly feminine, positive, domestic, and sexual. Similarly, the men of *Murderball* are cast as normal because of their associations with heteronormative masculinity: they are strong, violent, and full of machismo. Finally, while "real-life" portrayals move the freak body closer to Bakhtin's notion of the carnival, their place on screen limits their ability to recreate the freak show because the relationship between viewer and freak is still marked by a separation, both onscreen and between viewer and object. This separation becomes tenuous in the discussion of porn that follows in Chap. 5, and is finally undone in the discussion of Marilyn Manson and Lady Gaga of Chap. 6.

## CHAPTER 5

# Freak Pornography and the Cultural Politics of Disabled Sexuality

The lack of mediation in amateur pornography brings the viewer closer to the freakish body than ever before. Because there is no director, no crew, and no production company in amateur porn, which is nowadays mostly filmed on video cameras and on cell phones, there is little mediation in the genre. What you see is what you get. The realism of amateur pornography is so severe, in fact, that it becomes almost comical at times. In one particular video, for example, a disabled woman who is filming herself masturbating stops multiple times because she is interrupted by her child, her phone ringing, and a knock at the door. There are no edits and no cut-scenes, just awkward pauses. The viewer is so present that they even get to see what goes on behind the scenes. Of course, because the viewer is still watching from their computers, tablets, or phones, the spatial and temporal separation that is consistent in the new American freak show is present and accounted for. Though this may be the closest the viewer can get to the freak body without actually seeing it live and in the flesh, the viewer remains separated by space and time.

This short chapter picks up the reality and gender frameworks of the previous chapter and traces them through disability pornography including BDSM (BDSM includes bondage and discipline [B&D], dominance and submission [D&S], and sadism & masochism [S&M]) and amputee pornography. As discussed in Chap. 4, reality television attempts to lift the curtain on the freak show in order to see real freak sexuality, but fails because of its collision with heteronormativity

115

J.L. Williams, *Media, Performative Identity, and the New American Freak Show*, DOI 10.1007/978-3-319-66462-0_5

as well as through the mediation of documentary as a genre. Where reality television fails, however, disability pornography succeeds. Not only is the veil lifted, but the portrayals of disability and sex are at their most authentic because, while staged, they are not truly mediated.

Sexual attraction, to the point of fetishization, to disabled bodies has itself been classified as a disorder and therefore, more than a mere fetishization of weakened bodies, disability pornography seems to suggest a disability and a freakishness within the body of the person attracted to disabled sex. This blurring of freak and non-freak bodies recalls my earlier discussion of horror and thus further situates the disabled body as an object of fear. Further, as Linda Williams will help to show, disability pornography is the ultimate "body genre," a site of extreme excess and degradation.

While disability pornography transfers the disabled body from a site of pain and horror into one of pleasure, representations of the sexual disabled body are generally quite negative and are often even grotesque. I explore this through the example of the documentary *Sick: The Life and Death of Bob Flanagan Supermasochist*, a film that merges the genres of documentary and pornography, and explores the relationship between sexual deviancy and illness. Flanagan's disabled sadomasochism and disability porn's complicated relationship to the disabled body bridge the gap to my final chapter, in which I suggest that the freak show has become a pervasive and unmovable part of American popular culture.

## Disability Pornography

While my discussions of *Push Girls* and *Murderball* in the previous chapter pick up on the sexual proclivities and sexual identities of people with disabilities, the documentaries are ultimately neutered versions rather than real sexual representations. They are valuable, certainly, but they are also ultimately "safe" explorations of disabled sexuality. As discussed in the previous chapter, in the freak show, representations of sexuality also play it safe: sex is often suggested but is never explicit. We see this in pairings such as the human skeleton and the fat woman or a giant paired with a midget. The heterosexual coupling of these opposing freak identities suggests an unfamiliar and subversive sexuality that resides in the mind of the viewer. We see another example of this sort of sexual suggestion, though a bit more explicit, in *Freaks* when the Hilton sisters are seen with their respective mates. When one of the sisters passionately kisses her fiancé, the other sister sighs with pleasure. This raises all kinds of questions about the combined sexual experiences of conjoined twins. Is sexual autonomy possible? Privacy certainly is not. Questions of consent also arise. Though these questions are not explicitly asked, the pleasurable sigh that accompanies her sister's kiss is enough to lead viewers in this direction.

Perhaps no freak show body has been eroticized more than the black female body whose exploitation has been recorded in travelogues and other literature as far back as the fourteenth century. More recently, as Thomas Fahy tells us: "The construction of African Americans as freakish and the Victorian commercialization of these images contributed to racial tensions, which reached a breaking point in the early twentieth century" (20). Some of this is manifested in the lynching photography of the mid-nineteenth and early twentieth centuries: "The violence and cruelty of these images ... is compounded by their commercialization and their place in many family photo albums" (Fahy 20). The popularity of lynching photography coincides with the popularity of freak photography in general and it would not have been uncommon to see "images [of] black and otherwise exotic or maimed bodies" alongside one another in albums (20–21). The black body was itself exoticized via "safe" staging:

> Freak shows and freak photography ... provided 'safety' through distance. They needed to contain difference because the image didn't go away; the freak was not killed. As a result, freak shows used various methods to establish a clear, comfortable distance between audience and spectacle. The racial exhibit relied on a barker's spiel to reinforce the spectacle's freakishness and to entice customers; a stage setting supported the freak's 'exotic' origins (e.g., rocks, shrubbery, sticks, scanty clothing, etc.); performances, such as crawling, growling, singing and dancing, demonstrating his/her racial and cultural inferiority; and pamphlets and photography sold during and after viewing to advertise and commemorate the occasion. (22)

Not only is a safe distance maintained between audience and spectacle, but the superiority of the all-white audiences was reaffirmed through the degradation of the black spectacles on stage. While most freak show scholarship categorizes these displays as being part of the "exotic" mode of presentation, I tend to agree with Niall Richardson's assertion that "undoubtedly underpinning much of this was also the 'erotic'" (6). He furthers that "The unbridled sexuality of the primitive savage; the hypnotic feminine wiles of the snake charmer and, most importantly, the erotic potential of the extreme body whether it be the 'world's fattest lady' or the 'hermaphrodite' were undoubted sources of titillation for the spectator" (6).

Indeed, many of the black "exotic" performances of the freak show had an underlying eroticism to them. Saartjie (Sara) Baartman, who performed under the name "Hottentot Venus," was a San woman who had *steatopygia*, a condition characterized solely by a large accumulation of fat on the buttocks, which "appears to have been the single feature of her anatomy sensational enough to bring out crowds to see her" (Lindfors 208). Saartjie, who was "displayed, treated, and conceptualized as little better than an animal" was often physically groped and assaulted while she performed on stage (210–211, 208). Her body became a site of spectacle and one of sexual taboo, a fact underscored by her complete lack of autonomy and physical freedom. A precursor to many of today's oversexualized and commodified black women, Baartman and her body signified the sort of sexual transgression that surrounded the freak show. The dark sexuality that Baartman embodied, along with her complete commodification, brings to mind "the current engendered commercialization of black women like the 'video vixen' (who allows a credit card to be slid between her buttocks in Nelly's video Tip Drill, for example), and/or the sexualized female athlete: Serena Williams (crotch and butt shots), or the late track star Flo-Jo (nails, hair, body)" (Henderson 951).

The black body is not the only body that has been freaked and sexualized via the freak show model. In fact, sexual curiosity was an implicit part of the freak show. As discussed throughout previous chapters, the freak body often suggests a lack or an excess that is sexually intriguing to viewers, whether it be, for example, too much fat or too few limbs. Audiences are mesmerized by bodies that differ from theirs and much of this has to do with sex. As suggested by the frequent staging of coupled freaks and the often fabricated and sometimes real marriages between them, viewers are curious about the sexual proclivities and private lives of freak bodies. As Elizabeth Grosz posits, "it is not gross deformity alone that is so unsettling and fascinating. Rather, there are other reasons for this curiosity and horror" (64). Grosz furthers that "the initial reaction to the freakish and the monstrous is a perverse kind of sexual curiosity. People think to themselves: 'How do they do *it*?' What kind of sex lives are available to Siamese twins, hermaphrodites, bearded ladies, and midgets? There is a certain morbid speculation about what it would be like to be with such persons, or worse, to be them" (64).

And indeed, there is a morbidity, a horror element, to the sexualization of freakish bodies: "The perverse pleasure of voyeurism and identification is counterbalanced by horror at the blurring of identities (sexual, corporeal, personal) that witness our chaotic and insecure identities. Freaks traverse the very boundaries that secure the 'normal' subject in its given identity and sexuality" (Grosz 64). The freak body, such as that of the hermaphrodite or the (likely gaffed) Victor/Victoria, is doubled, blurred, or inherently contradictory in ways that reinforce our own corporeal instability. As such, when viewers look at such bodies we see a distorted mirror image that is both unsettling and fascinating.

As discussed in the previous chapter, we have seen that disabled bodies have historically been seen as non-sexual bodies, bodies that lack sexual desire or are sexually impotent. In addition, because of the disabled body's tendency to become a medicalized body, seeing it as a site of pleasure may seem like a foreign concept to some. As Tobin Siebers notes: "Disabled people have long struggled to take control of their bodies from medical authorities and to gain access to built environments and public institutions ... [D]isabled people experience sexual repression, possess little or no sexual autonomy, and tolerate institutional and legal restrictions on their intimate conduct" ("A Sexual Culture for Disabled People" 38). Alexa Schriempf discusses the example of a young woman with spina bifida who has dual fears about her ability to have a satisfying sex life because "(a) no one will see her as a fully adult (and therefore a sexual) woman and (b) her impairment will make sex difficult or unpleasurable" (54). Such preconceptions are commonly faced by both men and women with disabilities.

It follows that pornography of people with disabilities is an understudied area because "it is commonly assumed that they are rarely portrayed as sexual beings" (Elman 193). Perhaps the most prominent reason for the lack of sexual representation for people with disabilities is that the disabled body is viewed as being unattractive and thus not suitable for sexual intimacy. Richardson points out that the disabled body has been seen an unattractive for two primary reasons: that it reminds the "temporarily able-bodied" of their own fragility and ability to become disabled themselves, and secondly, that the disabled body does not stack up against traditional standards of beauty and, in fact, challenges those standards (193). While standards of beauty are constantly changing, the disabled body has remained static in its undesirability.

The *paraphilia*, or abnormal sexual attraction, to people with disabilities or deformities, has been classified as *teratophilia*. Speaking to this notion, Alison Kafer, author of "Desire and Disgust: My Ambivalent Adventures in Devoteeism" and double amputee, discusses the troubling relationship she has to the culture of men who are attracted to women with disabilities, noting that such attraction made her feel as if only a select few found her body attractive, as opposed to disgusting, and that these people seemed secretive and ashamed about their attraction to women with disabilities (333). This underscores the common perception that to be sexually attracted to a person with disabilities is a deviant and morally abhorrent act. She notes that "[u]ntil very recently, medical journals contained the only analyses of [sexual attraction to people with disabilities], analyses that relied heavily on the notion that a desire for disabled women is a pathological trait requiring therapeutic intervention" (333).

The classification of attraction to disabled bodies as pathological suggests more than a fetishization of vulnerable bodies. In fact, it suggests another blurring between the bodies of the abled and disabled. Who, in such a sexual relationship, is the freak? Is it the person with the disability who is engaging in a sex act (is s/he freakish for having sex?) or is it the person fetishizing the disabled body (is s/he freakish for wanting to have sex with someone because they are disabled)? The horror that arises in such a sexual union is due to this blurring—because we don't know who the freak is, we can't identify either body as normal. Through porn, disabled bodies become freak bodies, but so do the bodies attracted to disability.

Pornography can be defined as "any medium that depicts erotic behavior for the sake of sexual arousal" (Nord 185). Disability pornography is a genre of pornography that is certainly subversive yet surprisingly popular. In disability pornography, "people with physical disabilities play characters with disabilities, those with amputated limbs, who use wheelchairs, or who have vision impairment; however, people without disabilities have also been cast to play characters with disabilities" (Nord 185). Elman notes that "because disabled women and girls inherit ascriptions of passivity and weakness, pornographers and others have sometimes selected to portray them as the ultimate, compliant sex objects" (193). This places the disabled woman (and almost all of the subjects of disability porn are women [Nord 185]) in a vulnerable and tentative space: "Stated simply, through pornography, sexual abuse is decontextualized as assaultive and reconstituted as art and/or entertainment" (Elman 194). Whether or not all or even most disability porn is assaultive or should be considered abuse is an unanswerable question, but it is important to note the passive and degrading ways in which disabled women in porn are represented. Elman provides us with some examples:

> The American *Playboy* had a woman pose with her legs spread. She was in a plaster leg cast. Some time later, another woman appeared in a wheel chair. It seemed to some that *Playboy* was pursuing an agenda at odds with its promotion of the pornographic stereotype, liberating disabled women from the stigma of asexuality and/or sexual unattractiveness. Yet, pornographers have never promoted sexual liberation *for women*. Their sexualization of women's passivity and immobility, its fetishization and marketing, shows that such representations are entirely consistent with the central values of pornography. They are just one version of sexualized vulnerability. (Elman 194)

As Schriempf also points out, speaking of the same latter example, the woman in the wheelchair, Ellen Stohl, is either portrayed non-sexually with her wheelchair, or in sexually suggestive ways without it: "the two aspects of herself are neatly divided" (56). While disability porn may seem, at face value, to be empowering or mobilizing for women with disabilities, it is important to remember, as Elman notes, that the porn industry has never concerned itself with "promot[ing] sexual liberation *for women*" and that the vulnerability of this particular population is in fact being exploited. In other words, inclusion gets mistaken for representation here; just because women with disabilities are being included, does not mean that they are being represented.

In fact, I would argue that most, if not all disability pornography is exploitative. While pornography, in general, tends toward the exploitation of women, I do believe that pornography can be empowering to some women, both the women who star in pornography and female viewers. Particularly because of the changing viewership of pornography to include far more women than in years past, but also because of the current vastness and wide-ranging subject matter of pornography, porn has become more inclusive and depicts women in a wider array of roles than ever before. Just because a woman's naked body may be on display, does not necessarily mean that she is being exploited. In disability pornography, however, the woman's body is always a compromised body and the porn is therefore always exploitative because the women's bodies are by default weakened, victimized, and fetishized. Even when the disabled bodies on display are male, the females engaging disabled men in sex are seen as monstrous, slutty, or domineering in particularly negative ways.

Linda Williams' "Film Bodies: Gender, Genre, and Excess," an important essay in terms of this discussion, deliberates what Williams refers to as the "body genres" of horror, pornography, and the woman's "weepie" or melodrama. Her concept of the body genre helps us to further theorize the disabled body in pornography as the ultimate "body genre" and as an object of horror and patriarchal oppression. Her essay "explores the notion that there may be some value in thinking about the form, function, and system of seemingly gratuitous excesses in these three genres" (3). She argues for "the need to recognize the possibility that excess may itself be organized as a system" and notes that despite this fact, "analyses of systems of excess have been much slower to emerge in the genres whose non-linear spectacles have centered more directly upon the gross display of the human body" (3). She names pornography and horror as two of these systems of excess, noting that "[p]ornography is the lowest in cultural esteem, gross-out horror is next to lowest"—probable reasons for the lack of attention they have received (3). I would argue that disability pornography, a genre which straddles the border between horror and pornography, could be the lowest genre in terms of societal value. In disability pornography, like horror, "identification seems to oscillate between powerlessness and power" ("Film Bodies" 8), and disability pornography, again like horror, is filled with images of the "ruined," "incomplete," "damaged," or otherwise "monstrous body" on display in ways far beyond what is seen in the horror genre. In disability porn, full access is given to the disabled body; in it, we see all that horror (and the freak show) have not allowed us to see, and more. In some ways, disability pornography actually solves one of the problems of the freak show— the desire to see all is fulfilled through disability porn.

Williams characterizes her three body genres as being "featured most sensationally in pornography's portrayal of orgasm, in horror's portrayal of violence and terror, and in melodrama's portrayal of weeping" (4). Because disability pornography *is* pornography, first and foremost, it is perfectly situated under Williams' definition, but it also fits under her characterizations of horror and melodrama too, if not as neatly. That most pornography is implicitly violent might go without saying, but because of the disabled body being situated as a monstrous body in disability porn, and because of its penchant for BDSM, disability porn is a particularly violent type of pornography, as addressed above. Finally, while the woman's weepie, or melodrama, that Williams discusses is characterized in part by a display of emotion, manifested in tears, we can see the disabled woman in pornography as being "under patriarchy"—"as wives, mothers, abandoned lovers, or in their traditional status as bodily hysteria or excess" (4)—as all women in pornography arguably are, and thus we can further classify disability porn as the ultimate "body genre," a particularly embodied horror, pornography, and melodrama.

One of the most popular subgenres of disability pornography is amputee porn, a highly visible fetishization of the disabled female body. Consumers of amputee porn often call themselves "devotees" and "fetishists," although they are clinically referred to as *acrotomophiles* (Elman 197). Sexologists John Money and Kent W. Simcoe explain, "An acrotomophile is erotically exited by the stump or stumps of the amputee partner, and is dependent on them for erotosexual arousal and the facilitation or attainment or orgasm'" (qtd. in Elman 197). Based on the rare demographic analysis of devotees as well as anecdotal evidence, Kafer classifies devotees as being "white, middle- to upper-middle class, well-educated men between the ages of twenty-five and sixty-five" (335).

Devotees are known for some questionable behavior including harassment, stalking, and even "attending and sometimes organizing disability-related events, [and] lurking in public places to watch, take covert pictures of, talk to and touch disabled persons'" (Elman 197–198). The power dynamic implicit in a sexual relationship between disabled and able-bodied persons is more generally, of course, also problematic:

> It is very easy to say that if a man finds a quadriplegic female body to be attractive then he is eroticizing the power dynamic he can wield over her. She is vulnerable, dependent upon her wheelchair for mobility and, in many ways, subservient to him. If a man eroticises female disability he, arguably, eroticises the vulnerability of that body and his potential mastery of his sexual partner. (Richardson 195)

This brings to mind a storyline from *Push Girls* in which Tiphany recounts the dangers of dating while female and disabled. One story that stands out as being particularly horrifying is that of a man tipping Tiphany over in her wheelchair while out on a date with her, thus exploiting her vulnerability and putting her in real danger.

I think Richardson is correct in asking "whether desire for physical characteristics can ever truly be separated from social connotations ... *can* a body signify outside of its social setting?" (Richardson 197). As an attempted response, I would say that within a devotee's private relationship with an amputee, there certainly can be a separation between the disability and its social connotations. However, in disability pornography in particular, the social stigmas are indisputably present. Disability pornography tends to take on one of two extremes: either the amputee is a submissive vessel for the amputation itself, or she is a dominating force who is often "castrating, dominant and violent (Elman 198). In both situations, "pleasure derives particularly from their disability" (Elman 198).

All of the amputee porn on Porn Hub, a popular amateur pornography website, features amputee women performing in sex acts alone or with men; not surprisingly, there are no male amputees shown. Most of the videos are, unexpectedly, pretty tame when it comes to depicting disability. They are all very run-of-the-mill porn videos that just happen to feature female amputees. And while their stumps are prominently displayed, they are not the focus of the sex acts themselves. In "Quad Amputee Beauty," a nine-minute video with over 23,000 views,[1] there is actually no sex or nudity at all. Rather, the woman in the video poses in various positions on a couch, her stumps on full display, as her picture is taken. Similarly, in "Quad Amputee," a video with over 3000 views, a young woman, Amy, spends over eighteen minutes demonstrating how she works out with no arms or legs. Again, there is no nudity or sex in the video. That these videos are featured on a porn website, and yet are not pornography at all, suggests that there is something implicitly pornographic, and even horrific, about looking at the disabled female body.

Another excellent example is a video called "Amputee Sex," which does not actually feature any sex or nudity at all. The 37-minute clip follows a woman, Elena, through her morning routine of lounging in bed, brushing her hair, taking a bath (though her naked body is covered by bubbles), painting her toenails, eating breakfast, and getting dressed. The video, which has upwards of 22,000 views, suggests that, as in the freak show, viewers want to see people with disabilities performing everyday tasks. "Amputee Sex" is reminiscent of the opening faux-documentary scenes in *Freaks* in which we view various freak bodies doing common

---

[1] All view counts are as of May 2017.

daily things like eating and smoking cigarettes. This underscores the idea that, even without sex, the disabled body is seen as a subversive and problematic body.

The most interesting part of the video happens over twenty minutes in: after her bath, Elena lotions her leg and then her stump. When she rubs the lotion onto her stump, the camera zooms in and focuses on her massaging her stump for an extended time. She squeezes, caresses, and massages it in an erotic way; it is almost masturbatory. This scene is the only moment that is sexual in nature in the video and it is one of the only videos on Porn Hub that feature the site of disability so prominently.

One exception, "Amputee Sucking," shows multiple women with double arm amputations fellating what appears to be the same man. In each of the scenes, the man holds the head of the woman firmly and essentially fucks her mouth while she chokes, gags, and spits out his semen. Because she has no arms and he is holding her head, she has no control over the depth or intensity of the act and is used as a mere prop or vessel to get him off. Another exception is found in the comment sections, which actually might provide the most insight into who the audience for these videos is. On "Punk Amputee...," a fairly tame video of a punk couple having sex, some of the comments are quite interesting, particularly those with requests for future videos. One user says, "I love little short of your fingers and lovely stump ... If possible, I'd like to have some more of your [disabled] hands" [sic] while another says, "Still wanna see him cum on your stumps."

More subversive videos can be found on lesser-known websites such as xvideos.com. In "Lesbian Amputee Little Arm Love," for example, two women engage in sexual activities that include one woman licking and fellating the other's arm stump, followed by the disabled woman penetrating the other woman with her arm stump to orgasm. Paid sites, such as rawhandicapsex.com, offer even more kink. Many of these videos do, in fact, highlight the disabled body as part of the sex act, such as in "Handicap Amputee Porn with Half a Leg Screws a Hooker," which begins with the prostitute using the disabled man's prosthesis to masturbate while he watches and pleasures himself.

The site also shows quite a lot of men with disabilities at the center of its videos. The overarching narrative of these videos seems to be about either a prostitute or other personified vixen/slut who can't get enough of the disability (usually but not always an amputation). The man does not particularly appear to be in control in many of these videos. Even when using his stump to masturbate the woman, as in "Harlot Rubs Stumps On Her Tits And Pussy," she holds and directs his stump. Thus, he isn't getting her off but rather she's using his body to get herself off. Despite the woman's control, she is still demeaned via her identification as a whore or a slut. The descriptions of the videos, in particular, underscore this. From "Handicap Amputee Porn with Half a Leg Screws a Hooker":

> A lot of guys like this gentlemen, who is missing part of this leg [sic], are still lusty males who need satisfaction, but of course what chick would want to fuck them? ... Despite missing his leg, he can still pound a bitch good, giving it to her in a hard doggy and then missionary fuck.

What's interesting here is that the man is both emasculated ("what chick would want to fuck them?"; he must rely on a prostitute, etc.) and masculinized (he can "pound a bitch good" despite his disability), suggesting that maleness and disability are at once contradictory and superfluous.

It should not go without noting that there appears to be a connection between disability porn and death. In horror, Williams argues that "killing functions as a substitute for rape" ("Power, Pleasure, and Perversion" 40), so it might follow that in disability porn, a genre that appears to be situated on the border of horror, fucking functions as a substitute for death. In both, we see a literal or metaphorical "opening" of the body, whether it be the phallic knife opening the body with its repeated stabs in horror, or the amputated leg being removed and used as a masturbatory tool in disability porn. Disability and death are, in many ways, bedfellows, so it could follow that to seduce and sexually engage with one is a passage to the other. Bazin's notion of orgasm as "the little death" is not irrelevant here; if to cum is to die, if "death is the negative equivalent of sexual pleasure" (Williams "Power, Pleasure, and Perversion" 38) then to sexually engage with a body that is culturally constructed as being closer to death, a disabled body, seems to be a way to safely test one's mortality, to touch death and survive to tell the tale.

We have seen how fetishizing disability is often seen as perverse, but I wonder if it is more complex than mere sexual dysfunction. Perhaps, fetishizing disability is akin to inspiration porn. The term has been popularized by disability activist Stella Young, and is defined by Jan Grue as "the representation of disability as a desirable but undesired characteristic, usually by showing impairment as a visually or symbolically distinct biophysical deficit in one person, a deficit that can and must be overcome through the display of physical prowess" (838). Young herself explains the term as "an image of disability, often a kid, doing something completely ordinary—like playing, or talking, or running, or drawing a picture, or hitting a tennis ball—carrying a caption like 'your excuse is invalid' or 'before you quit, try' (qtd. in Grue 839). The term itself does not refer to actual porn; the idea is that viewers or consumers of such images are inspired and titillated by the representation of a person with a disability doing something ordinary. It fits nicely within the supercrip paradigm in which people with disabilities are seen as being extraordinary for doing ordinary things.

Actual pornography featuring people with disabilities then, can be seen as a type of inspiration porn. Having sex is, by its very nature, a primal yet completely ordinary act. The object of disability pornography is, like the object of inspiration porn, objectified, devalued, and mystified by the viewer. In her explanation of inspiration porn, Grue identifies the phenomena as problematic because of these three factors (840). In inspiration porn, "people with impairment are not represented as disabled subjects, but as objects. The audience is implicitly or explicitly assumed not to have impairment, and there is little ground for identification between the two" (840). Similarly, in disability porn, the partner of the disabled person, who is clearly objectified—nothing more than a disability—is always able-bodied and the only middle ground between the two is the seemingly shared sexual interest in the disabled body.

Next, she speaks to the devaluation of the disabled body in inspiration porn, stating that "[t]he achievements depicted in inspiration porn may be commonplace acts (e.g. walking on prosthetic legs). People with impairment are thus represented as having a smaller scope for achievement than is the case" (840). Surely, the act of having sex is a commonplace, everyday experience for many people. The fact that a sex act is not seen as ordinary for a person with a disability only furthers disability porn as a type of inspiration porn. The disabled person is extraordinary for engaging in sex acts, particularly with an able-bodied partner. Finally, Grue comments on the individualization and mystification of inspiration porn when she says: "Because of its focus on visible impairment and physical prowess, inspiration porn represents disability as a problem located in individual bodies, to be overcome through individual efforts"

(840). She furthers states: "By constructing disability as an objectively available, visually distinct, individual impairment, inspiration porn obscures structural and systemic causes of disability" (840). Likewise, disability pornography is almost solely focused on the visible impairment—it is the sole reason for the sex act to take place. If it were not for the disability, devotees would not be interested in the same woman's body. The disability, then, is a "problem located in individual bodies," (840) though in this case it is not to be overcome but to be worshiped and, it could also be argued, act as a source of inspiration.

## Bob Flanagan, Supermasochist

*Sick, the Life and Death of Bob Flanagan, Supermasochist*, reminiscent of disability porn itself, begins with a montage of close-up images of Flanagan's face that represent, simultaneously, sex and sickness. We see him writhing in what could equally be pleasure or agony, getting hit in the face with pies (a sexual innuendo, certainly), being blindfolded and gagged with a ball gag, possibly urinated on, getting slapped, having what appears to be semen poured on his face, and fellating various phallic objects. Before his death at the age of 43 in 1996, the performance artist was one of the oldest living people with cystic fibrosis, or CF, a "hereditary disease that causes the body to produce an excessive amount of thick, sticky mucus which clogs the air passages of the lungs, making it difficult to breathe and causing repeated lung infection" (*Sick*) and his illness was the primary subject of his various performance pieces. For example, in one of his art pieces, "Visible Man," Flanagan creates a miniature version of himself in skeletal form, which focuses on his primary bodily excrements: mucus, semen, and feces. He infuses the Invisible Man with various household products to make it appear as if it is excreting these. While doing so, he details what his own mucus, semen, and feces look like.

Much of what he describes in the film is a consensual and healthy sadomasochistic (SM) relationship that he has with his partner, Sheree Rose. What concerns me is not his SM relationship itself, but rather the way his "sexual deviancy" (what Flanagan himself refers to as, and what I will refer to as his "sickness") overlaps with his disability (what I will refer to as his illness) (see Fig. 5.1). As McRuer notes, "Flanagan repeatedly affirmed that a range of meaning might be detected in his writings and performances" (183), a comment with which I strongly agree.

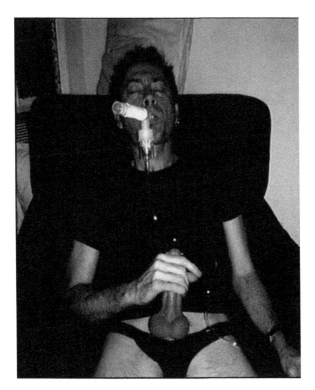

**Fig. 5.1**  Bob Flanagan, collision of "sickness" and "illness" in *Sick* (Dick 1997)

Flanagan's performances and sexual identity can be read in a variety of ways, some of which I explore below, but in almost all cases his sickness and illness are intrinsically linked.

Certainly, it is odd to see a person with a disability involved in sex acts to any extent. It is indeed rare to see such an overtly sexualized male with a disability. As Flanagan's "Make a Wish" visitor Sara says, "You don't hear about people with diseases being like that [sexual and/or sexually "perverse"]. You always think of them as being sick and feeble, ya know? And they don't really do anything" (*Sick*). But, as Reynolds points out, BDSM can offer a level of relief and control for people with disabilities:

BDSM is an important potential mode of personal empowerment for people with disabilities, because it represents a sexual community that accommodates different bodies and alternative lifestyles. In addition, BDSM plays with the unstable boundary between pain and pleasure, an issue that affects many people with disabilities, particularly those living with chronic pain.

...

BDSM plays with the unstable boundaries between pain and pleasure, an issue with which all people struggle—particularly those living with chronic pain. In addition, the philosophical aims of the BDSM community require negotiations to maintain a safe sexual practice. This approach maximizes the likelihood that practitioners can articulate their unique needs and that these needs will in fact be met. (40, 42)

However, in particular, men with disabilities have traditionally been seen as symbolically castrated, weak, and dependent on others so a person with a disability who is involved in BDSM appears to be a contradiction.

In addition, it is important to note that in his relationship with Sheree, Bob is the typically feminine submissive or "bottom" to Sheree's dominant or "top." It is true that female submissives are much more prevalent in hardcore pornography than their male counterparts. Linda Williams attributes this to "taboos against male homosexuality that operate with special force in genres of visual pornography segregated according to heterosexual or homosexual address to viewers" ("Power, Pleasure, and Perversion" 46). On the other hand, while it is true that Flanagan serves as the submissive in his relationship with Sheree, the bodily torture he endures takes a certain level of control, strength, and endurance that we do not typically imagine disabled men to have. As such, Flanagan's sick body (sick in both senses of the term) is a subversive body because it confronts taboos both about disabled men, and about sex and disability.

Viewers, at times, see Bob do "sick" things, like when he nails his penis to a board and then watches it bleed all over the camera lens, but we *always* see Bob being ill. At the very least, his nasal cannula is almost always on his face and he coughs quite frequently. In other words, Bob's illness is ever-present even when his sexual perversion, his sickness, is not. In fact, "During the course of [all of] his performances, Flanagan physically embodied his illness while he transcended the depiction of sickness he represented" (Reynolds 47). Ultimately, however, I think it is the collision of Flanagan's sickness and illness which make his body freakish, much like in the horror genre. If he were just sexually perverse, his would be a subversive body but not a particularly notable one. Plenty of people participate in BDSM relationships and many such exploits are heavily represented in porn and even in literature. Similarly, were Bob's body just a disabled body, he would again be unremarkable. His freakishness resides at the intersection of sick and ill because society tends to think of these identities either as oppositional or redundant. As McRuer notes, "Flanagan repeatedly drew attention to how his life interrupted classic disability narratives more generally and the standard narrative of CF, in particular" (187). His body undoes narratives about what it is like to be a male with a disability.

The fact that he is both sick and ill becomes almost redundant if we think of the ways in which the horror monster is sexually dysfunctional in some way. Describing what sounds like a monstrous body, Flanagan himself notes that "with all [his] heart and soul" he wants his body to be:

> strung up, spanked, splayed, saddled, stuck, strangled, split open, spread eagled, shit on, spat at, sewn up, shoved, shackled, shaved, shocked, sucked, sapped, soaked, screwed, stripped, scratched, suffocated, sacrificed, straight jacketed, squelched, stifled, scorched, straddled, stoned, smothered, smashed, screamed at, shouted at, snapped in two, sawed in half, stamped on, sat on, sodomized, stuffed, starved, strapped, stretched, submerged, surrounded, slugged, socked, scarred, skewered, slaughtered, stung, struck, slapped, slammed, sutured, swept up, saturated, savaged, seduced, stroked, and spent. (*Sick*)

Most of these descriptions, a merging of horror and pornography, could easily be applied to the monstrous body in horror. Here, Flanagan is monstrous in his male disability, his illness, and the ways in which the two intersect.

The baseness of Bob's body is interesting because, through torture, it becomes a site of horror rather than one of titillation. Flanagan provides a good example: "I went into the bathroom and with the claw of the hammer pulled the nail out [of his penis] and naturally a lot of blood gushed out. I was bleeding all over the bathtub; I turned the water on and bloody water was swirling down the drain just like in *Psycho*. I *felt* just like Tony Perkins" (Juno and Vale 22). Because it is tortured, in many of the ways described above, Bob's penis and his body become representative of abject, dysfunctional, and monstrous sexuality. It is the tortured body, the horror body, which Flanagan depicts time and again.

As Linda Williams notes in "Power, Pleasure, and Perversion: Sadomasochistic Film Pornography," there is both a temporal and spatial distance between the viewer and the object of pornography (as in all of the modes which I have been discussing) (38). Much like in the freak show, viewers maintain a safe distance through the "screens" that come between them and the bodies on display. However, the viewer is still affected; harm is done to both "individuals whose bodies are used to create these images" as well as "possible harm done to viewers," addressing the idea of "*cinema as perversion*" (38). Because the images viewed are both extremely sexual and violent, and because they illicit such strong responses in viewers, "we thus encounter a double perversion: perverse acts and the perverse pleasure of viewing these acts" (38).

Thus, the viewing body becomes perverse as well. Linda Williams invokes André Bazin's ontology of the photographic image in order to illustrate that "the filmic representation of an 'actual person' engaged in sexual acts is exactly the same as if witnessed 'in the flesh.' Thus, ... film audiences bear 'direct' witness to any violence or perversion therein enacted" (37). Therefore, viewers are assaulted via Flanagan's sick body, his "radical crip images," (McRuer 182) which are all the viewer has to look at throughout much of the documentary. This confuses ideas of perversion and sickness; if the viewer is bearing "direct witness," then they become complicit in the acts being performed and the images being viewed and are thus perverted and made monstrous via their viewing. If realism is equivalent to obscenity, as in Williams and Bazin, then viewing perverted depictions of disability is itself a monstrous act.

Flanagan also represents the medical model of disability, a paradigm which "rests on notions of *normality* and the dichotomy between normal and pathological" (Lewis 116). The medical paradigm, in other words, places the concentration on the disability rather than the person with the disability, and sees the disabled body as something to be remedied or fixed. We see this model perpetuated in *Sick* via the hospital and other medical imagery surrounding Flanagan throughout the documentary (see Fig. 5.2). Images of Flanagan surrounded by medical equipment abound in both the documentary and in his artwork. He performs in a hospital gown, he is seen using warm compresses, syringes, medical gloves, and an oxygen mask, and he even takes medical objects and turns them into sex toys (such as his butt plug medical stool). These images, when combined with his SM relationship with Sheree, work to medicalize the sex act.

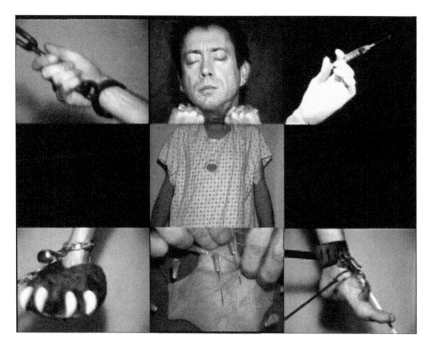

**Fig. 5.2**  Bob Flanagan, "The Scaffold," 1991 from *Sick* (Dick 1997)

In particular, Flanagan's 1994 New Museum of Contemporary Art installation "Visiting Hours" sees Bob's body as a medicalized body. Reynolds describes the installation as offering "several interactive exhibits containing props that audience members could physically handle or manipulate. Many of these exhibits spoke to the horrors Flanagan endured as a result of CF" (45). The art exhibit, which was envisioned as a pediatric medical ward, showcased much of Flanagan's work, but at the center was a performance piece in which Flanagan lay in a hospital bed and allowed the museum's guests to visit with him. Flanagan in the hospital bed is much like a freak on a stage but, in this instance, he is not freaked for his subversive sex life—he is fully clothed and in a non-sexual setting—yet his body still remains on display, freakish because of his illness. In his other pieces, his sex acts are represented all around him but they are separated, here, from his disabled body which is, in and of itself, a spectacle.

Speaking about "Visiting Hours," Reynolds argues that

> Flanagan's popular museum exhibit ruptures images of the disabled
> body as weak, asexual, and hidden from public view ... By embracing the
> negative stereotypes of disabled bodies, Flanagan played with these pre-
> conceived notions in ways that revealed their distorted (and, at times,
> humorous) realities ... Flanagan's inverted sexual role as master over his
> own illness and pain, if only for a moment, further illustrated the ways in
> which he plays with the concept of sickness. (Reynolds 41)

While I agree in part, I contend that Bob's performance piece resides
in its own separate space. While the rest of his exhibit certainly rejects
negative stereotypes of disability, Flanagan's ill body in a hospital setting
reinforces the binaries of sickness and health. Heathy visitors pay the ill
Bob a visit, possibly after sitting in the accompanying "waiting room"
he designed, speak to him about his illness, and ask him how he is feeling. Perhaps the crowd's desire to look at Bob's sick body is a way for
them to understand their own bodies and mortality—a way to use pornographic imagery to touch death. Or, as McRuer notes, "bad girls and sick
boys (or sick girls and bad boys) are also invariably subject to a diagnostic
gaze that would determine what is causing their deviance" (185). In the
hospital bed, however, there is no perversion, no sign of Bob's BDSM
lifestyle; though it is literally just around the corner, his illness becomes
separated from his sickness. Even when, at the end of the performance,
Bob is bound and strung upside down by his ankles, revealing his nude
body, the image is more transcendent and macabre than it is sexual.

And, ultimately, we find that Flanagan's sickness and illness are not
as completely intertwined as Flanagan himself suggests. Much of the six
interviews Bob gives with Juno and Vale in their Re/Search book *Bob
Flanagan: Supermasochist,* focus more on his SM lifestyle and relationship with Sheree Rose than on his illness itself. Flanagan's SM experiences
seem to take center stage in his life as he readily admits that he would
give up his art career if he had to choose between it and his SM relationship. He even admits that because of the progression of his disease, his
entire SM lifestyle had to change in ways more suitable to his illness (Juno
and Vale 67). In the end, he became what Sheree refers to as a "medical
masochist"; the pleasure he once got from SM had to somehow be trans-
ferred to the medical procedures he endured (Juno and Vale 108).

However, his disability trumps his sickness in the end. There is a scene
in which Sheree films Bob on his 42nd birthday and he is feeling sick
and miserable, stating that he wishes he were dead. Sheree wants to give
him 42 spanks for his birthday, but Flanagan's illness supersedes the sex;

he's just not up to it, both literally and emotionally. Toward the end of the film, when Bob starts nearing the end of his life, he and Sheree argue about their relationship and how he won't submit to her anymore. She says that he is no longer a masochist because life has just "beat him down" too much. The pain from his disability is so extreme that he can't submit to any additional pain. In the end, Flanagan's body becomes merely a disabled body; he may have fought "sickness with sickness" (Juno and Vale 3) but in the end the former wins out.

Like many freaks before him, Bob's body is put on display even in death. Not only does his legacy live on—"the poster child from hell isn't good for the CF mythology, or any other disability mythology. Most dangerously, this anecdote suggests that an undead Flanagan might walk the earth and recruit others" (McRuer 189)—but his actual death is recorded and shown in the documentary as is his dead body, the fluid that was in his lungs, and his burial.

The ultimate question surrounding Flanagan's life may be *why?* Why does he choose to fight "sickness with sickness" instead of some other, arguably healthier or more "normal," outlet? Is he fighting back against his body, as his mother posits? Is this his way to be a man in a body that is otherwise emasculated via disability? Practically speaking, "BDSM may provide a welcome sexual reprieve from the pain that can accompany some impairments (i.e., physical manifestations of a disease or condition)" (Reynolds 42). However, there is also a clear element of control involved: "Through various tortures, Flanagan was able to gain physical and psychological control over a body that was frequently out of control. Flanagan's self-imposed restrictions and degradations served as an entertaining way to keep his reckless, unpredictable body in line" (Reynolds 43). As Flanagan himself notes, "I was *forced* to be in the medical world, so I turned that into something I could have control over instead of something that was controlling me" (Juno and Vale 11).

Flanagan's poem "Why?" provides us with an array of possible answers. In it, Bob attempts to answer why he has chosen such a public SM lifestyle. He gives some fairly straightforward answers in the piece, such as "Because it feels good; because it gives me an erection; because it makes me come," but also explores the ties his sickness has with his illness. He says, "because I'm sick; because there was so much sickness; because I say FUCK THE SICKNESS" (Juno and Vale 64). That Flanagan would have anger directed at his younger experiences, in particular, and his disease, more generally, makes sense. He describes "the humiliation of medical procedures [he'd] have to endure: being on this electronic table for two hours getting a barium enema while [he] was a kid ... you're just naked in front of people on this Frankenstein table, and they're turning you upside down and doing all these things to you" (Juno and Vale 87). Flanagan's horrific early experiences with his cystic fibrosis seem to have left an indelible mark on him and became entwined with sex at an early age. He talks about the pleasure he experiences in being tied to hospital beds, rubbing against the sheets to soothe his aching stomach and turning that act into a masturbatory experience, and even playing "slave/master" games with his cousins as children (Juno and Vale 12).

There are other reasons given in "Why?" such as "because my parents loved me more when I was suffering" and "because I learned to take my medicine; because I was a big boy for taking it" (Juno and Vale 65) that also clearly hearken back to childhood. Bob himself notes that "While horrible things were happening to me, I was getting extra love and attention, so the two contradictory feelings probably fused together...the horrible things happening to me were made into something better" (Juno and Vale 13). Clearly, illness and sex became linked at a young age and only developed as Flanagan grew older. Flanagan's obsession with his own phallus, and the clear link that his SM has to his childhood, are in line with Deleuze's notion that "masochism has its genesis in the male child's alliance with the powerful oral mother of the pregenital stage" ("Power, Pleasure, and Perversion" 52).

"Why" confirms that Flanagan's relationship with BDSM and his cystic fibrosis is complicated, complicit, and breaks down traditional stereotypes about people with disabilities. This is not a "classic disability overcoming narrative" (McRuer 186), nor is it a mere explaining away of perceived sexual deviancy. In fact, "'Why' implicitly insists that the key is not to be found and performatively demonstrates that the 'answers' will keep coming" (McRuer 185). Despite Juno and Vale's assertion that Flanagan's SM practices do not define him as a freak (6), I would assert that his cystic fibrosis, when combined with his sex practices do, in fact, enter him into a freak show tradition. While Bob's body and sexual practices are a far cry from the freak show's mere suggested sexuality, they do follow in the tradition of sensationalizing the disabled body in a way that suggests a performativity undergone for the sake of an audience. Flanagan puts his body on display and performs both his sickness and illness, doubly outside the norm, twice freaked.

## CHAPTER 6

# Born This Way? Pop Culture's Collision with the Freak of Nature

The freak show traditionally offered viewers an array of acts that were both authentic—fat ladies, conjoined twins, one-legged men—as well as culturally created and gaffed—African Savages, Circassian beauties, Barnum's Feejee Mermaid. All freaks were created, as previously discussed, in the sense that they did not become freaks until they were exhibited. However, there was a distinction between born freaks—a person whose "anomaly was the starting point for the exhibition"—and made freaks who were "perfectly normal except in the way they were presented" (Bogdan 234). In exhibiting both authentic and made freaks, managers and showmen put a lot of work into creating the freak show's veil of authenticity, though many audience members were dubious about whether or not what they were seeing was "the real thing."

Today, we contest the authenticity of the freak body but have yet to come up with a consensus about what an authentic portrayal ought to look like. The portrayals of freakishness in previous chapters have provided us with some options—the foreign other who we can attempt to normalize, the freaks whose freakishness can be overlooked if they reinstate other forms of cultural normalcy, the freak who is monstrous, the freak who needs our pity—but each of these representations highlight areas of tension between real and culturally constructed freakishness. Which, if any, of these portrayals are authentic? This debate highlights a hierarchy within the culture of the freak body, from the born freak to the pop artist who performs freakishness. These degrees of authenticity exist with respect to physical impairments (a botched plastic surgery

© The Author(s) 2017

J.L. Williams, *Media, Performative Identity, and the New American Freak Show*, DOI 10.1007/978-3-319-66462-0_6

versus limblessness) but also with respect to the process of socialization. Popular culture shows us the gray areas within the debate for authenticity and affords us the opportunity to examine constructed freakishness in its current cultural context. To this end, I examine how cultural freaks invest and mark their bodies and performances with appropriated imagery from natural freaks. Specifically, I explore the self-identification as freak through performers Marilyn Manson and Lady Gaga. I argue that these sites of culturally constructed freakishness showcase how ability, sexuality, and gender identities help shape cultural constructions of freakishness and therefore cannot be separated from freakish bodies.

Although appropriated freakishness can be positive and useful, and can show us things about the way we understand the presentation and viewing of public bodies, appropriated freakishness is unmasked when it comes into contact with real disability or more authentic freak bodies. However, it is in the blurring of normal and freakish within a single body—rather than the blurring of different normal and freakish bodies on screen—that produces real horror as well as brings the freak show back from the screen into the world of the traditional freak show. It is, in fact, bodies such as Manson and Gaga's that bridge the gap between the freak show and the viewing public.

## The Freak of Culture: An Act of Collision Within a Body

Both Marilyn Manson and Lady Gaga have embraced a constructed freakishness by portraying themselves as (temporarily) disabled in their acts and performances and by having publically identified as freak. By occupying the spaces of both live and recorded performances, these subjects occupy a unique position and are thus presented with distinctive struggles. We see Gaga and Manson live onstage, through the lens of the paparazzi, as well as in their music videos—all, to varying degrees, fictionalized performances even though some of these appear to be authentic or unperformed portrayals. Therefore, audiences see the bodies of these performers in conflicting contexts. Examining the ways they portray the freak body through different visual representations allows us a unique perspective into culturally constructed freakishness and allows us to see their freak bodies both mediated and in the flesh, a point that cannot be understated.

In horror, we have seen how the freak body is often feminized, complicated, and brought into contact with normal bodies in order to raise questions about normality, eliciting fear and self-reflection in audiences. In the visual culture surrounding the music industry and, more generally, celebrity culture in America, both the natural and made freak body often border on horror and the grotesque. Gaga will show us that the process of becoming disabled is often horrible, as is the physical spectacle of the disabled and grotesque body, which Manson also repeatedly demonstrates in his music videos. The nature of the internet allows us inside access into how audiences respond to this pop culture horror; fan message boards and blogs, in particular, offer us first-hand reactions to the portrayal of the popular freak spectacle.

I have said that all freaks are freaks of culture. By this, I mean that those with abnormalities and disabilities are not freaks until they are *made* freaks by being given an audience and a spectacular narrative, or by being objectified by viewers. As Bogdan notes, "All freaks were creations of the amusement world: the freak show and the presentation made people exhibits, not their physiology" (234). In other words, freakishness, like gender, is not an intrinsic quality, but rather a performative identity; it is something someone *does*, not something someone *is*.[1] Because freakishness can be considered socially constructed, the definition of who and what we consider freakish has changed, like most social constructions do. However, while freaks of nature can be considered freaks of culture, freaks of culture cannot be considered freaks of nature. This speaks to the hierarchy that is present both between freaks of nature and freaks of culture as well as within the range of freaks of culture: a person with a full body of tattoos versus a sword swallower, for example.

While the traditional freak show always had a mixture of freaks of nature and freaks of culture, the social and scientific advances of the twentieth century resulted in a decrease of the former and an increase in the latter. Bogdan suggests that although it was challenging for those who were not born freaks to become very successful, many did so. They fell into one of three distinct groups: those who were perfectly normal but were presented as rare or exotic, such as Circassian beauties, "genuine" Caucasian women of the "purest stock" in the world; those who

---

[1] I am referencing Judith Butler's notion of gender as a performative identity from her *Bodies that Matter*.

acquired their physical oddities, such as heavily pierced and tattooed men and women; and novelty acts who perform tricks such as eating glass, swallowing swords, or charming snakes (234–236). These performers were incredibly useful because they did not rely on special talent (novelty acts were easily learned), and were not dependent on a physical disability or deformity to perform their act. Hence, new freaks could be created and promoted on an as-needed basis.

While the self-made freak was an important piece of the traditional freak show, today the made freak *is* the freak show. With few exceptions, the freak shows that still exist today are comprised of novelty acts and heavily modified men and women. Of course, there are good reasons for this: progresses in prenatal care that have resulted in fewer cases of severely disabled infants; medical advances that healed or improved the lives of many with disabilities; social protests over the inhumanity of freak shows; and viewers' guilt about looking at abnormal bodies. Because a made freak becomes a freak by choice, it would follow that those on display in freak shows also willingly chose to be exhibited. On the other hand, many people simply could not believe that a person with a disability or impairment would ever choose to perform in a freak show (of course this was not the case as many performed willingly and happily). While it is fair to say that all freaks are socially constructed, a difference remains between someone who is born with a physical anomaly and someone who creates their own. As Mary Russo says, "Being a freak was, and remains, an individual choice for some and an oppressive assignment for others" (90). The difference, again, lies in the ability to choose. However, given the treatment of born freaks, one must question *why* someone would choose to display themselves in a way that would render them a freak in public.

Some answers can be found by turning again to a few examples from Dunn's *Geek Love*. One of the story's main threads is Arturo's ascension to become the founder of Arturism—the belief in all that Arturo, or Arty, preaches. His sermons are grounded in his family's beliefs that freaks are actually superior to norms. His followers live by what he preaches and want to be as he is—limbless. Arty hires a surgeon and the Arturians begin eliminating their body parts in devotion.

Arturo's preaching provides much insight into why people would want to freak themselves. Part of it seems very simply to be the desire to feel special and unique: "Hunger artists, fat folks, giants, and dog acts come and go but *real* freaks never lose their appeal" (Dunn 278). The logic of the Binewski family is that if one is a true freak, they will always be desired.[2] There is something in such a notion that could charm people who feel insignificant or uninteresting. As Olympia says, "Each of us is unique. We are masterpieces" (282). The same can be said of someone like the Lizardman, a frequent performer at Coney Island's freak shows, who has modified his body to resemble an amphibian, for instance.[3] In questioning the authenticity of his freakishness we must acknowledge that he was not physically born that way, but perhaps this suggests that freakishness is not always tangible, that it is sometimes a personality trait or something inherent in a person's character. In other words, the Lizardman's modified body is his inner freak made visible. In making himself a freak (a word he has tattooed across his chest), he is buying into the uniqueness that Olympia and the other Binewskis cherish so much because it makes them feel desirable.

Arturo's main line of reasoning for why people should amputate their limbs is that it allows for freedom from pain. When you are able-bodied you have to worry about what others think of you, you have standards to live up to, and other people to please. As a freak, you are free from all of this because society will not have any expectations of you. During his shows Arturo barks to his norm audiences, "I want you to be like I am! I want you to become what I am! I want you to enjoy the fearlessness that I have! The courage that I have! And the compassion that I have!" (190). According to Arturo, this is only possible through sacrificing the body. Like Leatherface and Hitchhiker, Arty's disabled body is at once a ruined body and a body that allows freedom from social expectations because it has been ruined. Therefore, being a freak places you outside of society's rules and standards. A new category is created but by definition holds less cultural stock and is separate from the mainstream.

Of course there are many other reasons why people freak themselves. The Lizardman considers his body part performance art and part social experiment (Sprague 8). Another freak performer, Mike Wilson, provides an interesting perspective: he similarly celebrates his body and says that

---

[2] Of course this raises the questions, What is a true freak or a real freak? Novelty acts are certainly not true freaks, but heavily modified bodies and Arty's followers are buying into a realer freakishness because they are making significant and permanent changes to their bodies.

[3] Freak performer Erik Sprague, "The Lizardman," a Coney Island regular, is also famous through his association with Ripley's Believe it or Not!

becoming heavily tattooed signifies "a possible way … for me to achieve a whole other frame of reference, and to elicit experiences beyond the 'normal'…presenting yourself as a signal beacon drawing things to happen to you" (Sprague qt. Wilson 7). For Wilson, becoming freak begets a more interesting life. Many self-freaking practices are deeply connected to sexuality and sexual pleasure. The documentary *Flesh and Blood* shows procedures such as penis splicing, testicle piercing, tongue bifurcation, corset piercing, and even more extraordinary modifications done both for aesthetic reasons and for increased sexual arousal. For many extreme modifiers, there is a level of physical pleasure involved in the process itself. For others, the body is modified to take sexual pleasure to a new level.

Just as we see so many teenagers rebel through their clothing and hairstyle choices, freaking the body in more permanent ways can be a subversive act. Media theorist Dick Hebdige examines how a person's style and the signifying objects attached to it can have subversive implications and can speak and rebel for us. For him, style can be used and read "as a form of Refusal" [sic] (2). While I am specifically discussing the freak body, Hebdige's argument about subcultures, objects (as signifiers, which express double meanings), and the exchanges that make these objects meaningful to both subcultures and the dominant culture, is helpful in explaining the draw to subversive styles and self-made freaks. As noted above, because freakishness is socially constructed, what is considered freakish is continually changing depending on time, location, and social context. Hebdige says that the meaning of subcultural style is "always in dispute." Subcultural style, because of its opposition to the majority, is "a gesture of defiance or contempt" that has substantial subversive value. Significantly, he notes that subcultural style is an "expression both of impotence and a type of power" (3). This means that the self-made freak has been marginalized by or rejected from the majority and thus the subversion is symbolic of a separation from the dominant culture. At the same time, however, the self-made freak is also empowering himself or herself because he or she has chosen to reject rather than assimilate into that dominant culture.

While the freaking of one's body is certainly not always a sign of perversion or suffering, popular explanations of self-made freaks often seem to propose this. This suggests that we are always looking for the horror and the pain in the freak body whether it is a born or constructed body. The performances of Manson and Gaga allow us to examine those moments of shock and horror in different contexts as well as urge us to question what lies behind such cultural reactions.

## THE BEAUTIFUL PEOPLE, THE HORRIBLE PEOPLE

Known more for his controversial stage performances, music videos, and outspokenness than for his music, Marilyn Manson (born Brian Warner) loomed over the 1990s like a bad dream. For many, Manson represented a threat to their values, children, and sense of normalcy. A self-pronounced Satanist, Manson quickly became known as a shock rocker, someone who would push the limits of decency while still straddling mainstream popularity. For most of his critics, he is simply too much of everything: too masculine, too feminine, too angry, too dark, too thin, too dangerous. He also appears to have too much of everything: too many tattoos, too many scars, too much body revealed, too many drugs consumed, too much power given to him both by fans and critics.

While few would consider Marilyn Manson a mainstream artist, his major label record deal, three Grammy nominations, numerous gold and platinum albums, and many arena tours suggest that he has, in fact, had a very commercially successful career. A lot of this success derived from word of mouth on the internet, which became available in the average American household around the time of Marilyn Manson's inception. During the 1990s, chat rooms and message boards were filled with Manson fans (calling themselves the Spooky Kids, after the band's original name, Marilyn Manson and the Spooky Kids) who were, for the first time, able to connect to like-minded outcasts almost anywhere in the modern world.

Gavin Baddeley, whose *Dissecting Marilyn Manson* is the sole book-length analysis on Manson, notes that the band was the first to really take advantage of the internet with Manson himself communicating with his fans regularly via his personal website (64). He has used his site as a means of connecting his fans to one another and to himself, saying that he and his fans should be "the biggest spider on the web" and that the internet should become *their* web, "[n]ot something that uses us, but something that we will control" (Baddeley qt. Manson 64). His website has undergone many reincarnations and today there are sites that host archives of each past version of it.[4]

---

[4] Such as "The Vault: The Complete Marilyn Manson Archives" at www.nachtkabarett.com.

The web has also become the most prosperous space for anti-Manson propaganda to circulate. Christian groups, for example, have used the internet to drum up anti-Manson support. One instance of this included circulating statements which were supposedly signed by those claiming that "underage teenagers had been seen handcuffed on the Manson tour bus, their faces later appearing on 'Missing' notices" (Baddeley 64). Acting as anti-hype for the band, these and other attempts to ruin Manson are like "300-foot-tall 'parental advisory' stickers in psychedelic neon" (8). In other words, something intended to keep teenagers away from Manson instead only succeeded in making the band appear more attractive to rebellious teens. If nothing else, for an artist whose act relies so heavily on the visual, the rise of the internet was essential to Manson's success as it allowed people to look at him and watch him perform as often as they pleased.

Even though Manson found his inspiration in listening to heavy metal while growing up in Canton, Ohio in the 1970s and '80s, and even though he is categorized by most as a heavy metal artist, Manson is not the stereotypical metal front man. One view of the metal persona is drawn out in Ryan Moore's positioning of the heavy metal movement alongside the deindustrialization of the 1970s and '80s. He refers to the time as a "crisis of masculinity," citing job loss, fear of unemployment, downward mobility, and the rise of the feminist movement as the precedents for the emasculation of the working-class male and the loss of the American male's breadwinner identity (80). Thus, heavy metal had a built-in audience waiting for it "among the first generation of working-class youth and masculine rebels who didn't have a factory job waiting for them when they left school, and who would therefore constitute a surplus population subject to intensified processes of social control" (81). He furthers that metal allowed young men to rediscover and reassert their masculinity through aggressive music, costumes, and a generally patriarchal and violent scene. For Moore, metal was the ultimate boys' club for the young white working-class.

The other popular image of metal comes later with the 1980s hair metal movement. Bands such as KISS, Mötley Crüe, and Poison are the most obvious and extreme examples. These bands introduced more gender blurring than was seen in more "hardcore" metal bands, although even many stereotypically hypermasculine metal bands performed wearing platform shoes, makeup, and long teased hair. However, the ambiguously gendered styles of metal performers were characteristically offset by the persistent presence of scantily clad women and exaggerated heterosexuality that surrounded such bands. In other words, even if they looked feminine, they always acted clearly hetero-masculine.

While Manson cites many of these bands as influences, especially KISS, but also Dio, Black Sabbath, Rainbow, Led Zeppelin, Alice Cooper, and Queen (*The Long Hard Road Out of Hell* 25–26), Manson, in his own public persona, has vacillated between the requisite masculine identity attached to the heavy metal movement and the gender ambiguity that many of his influences made popular. Manson has taken these two prototypes to an extreme, however, and has truly become the embodiment of his stage name.

As an entertainer, what Manson has looked like at any given time has had more social significance than his music. In the early 1990s, Manson was often costumed in ripped stockings and leather underwear with bright red lipstick, heavy black eyeliner, and mismatched colored contact lenses. There were often noticeable scars and open cuts on his body and his long black hair was straggly and untamed. Though his look has changed significantly and often over the years, each visual reincarnation of Manson has been similarly freakish. Other memorable looks include his *Mechanical Animals* era incarnation as a gender ambiguous alien and *The Golden Age of Grotesque* years in which he frequently wore Mickey Mouse ears and uniforms reminiscent of World War II Germany.

A self-proclaimed decadent, Manson has made a career out of going to extremes. Baddeley says that the description of decadence fits Manson "like a rubber dress" (15). He elaborates:

The decadents cultivated a fascination with all that was commonly perceived as unnatural or degenerate, with sexual perversity, nervous illness, crime, and disease, all presented in a highly aestheticized context calculated to subvert or ... to shock conventional morality ... Decadence is an aesthetic in which failure and decay are regarded as seductive, mystical, or beautiful...The typical decadent hero is ... a man whose masculinity is confounded by his tendency to androgyny, homosexuality, masochism, mysticism, or neurosis. (15)

Everything about Manson screams perversity and decadence. A sort of living horror film, Manson is a hybridized monster whose body blurs the boundaries between male and female, healthy and sickly, and natural and mechanical. His gender identity, in particular, seems to have no set parameters. His stage name combines the theoretical opposites of Marilyn Monroe, America's most beloved sex symbol, and Charles Manson, America's most feared criminal, into the persona of Marilyn Manson. As Manson himself has noted, "I thought that those two – positive/negative, male/female, good/evil, beauty/ugliness – created the perfect dichotomy of everything I wanted to represent" (Baddeley qt. Manson 7). Interestingly, Manson could just as well be referring to some of the horror villains examined in Chap. 3. Leatherface, for instance, parallels Manson's dual persona as he is both victim and monster, masculine and feminine, beautiful and ugly. With his serial-killer-meets-innocent-sex-icon stage name, Manson neatly places together the often opposing personalities found in horror monsters.

In embodying extremes, Manson and what could be called his performance art connect strongly to the freak show. Baddeley notes that Manson's persona "combines elements of traditional masculinity, like his aggressive stage performances, with characteristics traditionally associated with femininity, such as his flamboyant dress and make-up." Manson does not think of himself as a cross-dresser or a transvestite—he has been accused of both—but rather as "a composite of both male and female … something that *is* both" (92. My emphasis.) In doing so, Manson's body brings to mind the gender ambiguity at the heart of many freak show exhibits such as bearded women, hermaphrodites, and half-men/half-women. However, like Leatherface, Manson's masculinity shows through his costuming and identification as a hybrid gendered body. In other words, even when adopting a female image, it is a grotesquely masculine female image; he cannot completely undo his maleness, the characteristics of which seem almost to seep out into his persona. His ultimate classification as a powerful male is, in fact, what makes his self-made freakishness ultimately seem more authentic. This is ironic because Manson gains access to the freak body by blurring his gender identity but is authenticated as freak because of his ultimate positioning as a misogynistic male (a point I will return to in more detail below).

Beyond its gender ambiguity, the theatricality that is implicit in metal connects it even more clearly to the freak show tradition. Stage performances with fire-breathing, clownish makeup, self-injury, and pyrotechnics are characteristic of metal performances. Metal, then, is sort of a dark carnival that brings together extremes in exciting ways. Karen Bettez Halnon argues that Manson is a part of this "heavy metal carnival," a movement that she describes as a politics of grotesque realism (35).

Relying heavily on Mikhail Bakhtin's notions of the carnivalesque, Halnon positions Manson, among other metal acts such as Slipknot and Insane Clown Posse, as a modernized, heavy metal reincarnation of the medieval carnival. For Bakhtin, the grotesque is not simply the disgusting and obscene, but "an umbrella term for a comedic, satirical 'exaggeration of the improper,' an excessive and superabundant transgression of all limits" (Halnon 36). The grotesque sees the body as an earthly, malleable object that allows us to "suspend all conventions and established truths, to realize the relative nature of all that exists, and to enter a completely new order of things" (Bakhtin 34). The grotesque body in particular "transgresses the ordinary limits between self and the outer world" (Halnon 37). Bakhtin writes:

> Eating, drinking, defecation, and other elimination (sweating, blowing of the nose, sneezing), as well as copulation, pregnancy, dismemberment, swallowing up by another body—all these acts are performed on the confines of the body and the outer world, or on the confines of the old and new body.... The grotesque image displays not only the outward but also the inner features of the body: blood, bowels, heart and other organs. Its outward and inward features are often emerged into one. (317–318)

Bakhtin argues that the grotesque is not simply those "distasteful" things that are in or on the body, but rather that the grotesque image is often found in the process of exiting or entering the body. It is often a movement—a performed act—rather than a static image, in other words. It is no surprise, then, that the music video, in which one can perform and display such acts in both literal and metaphorical ways, would be an ideal outlet for someone like Marilyn Manson to explore the grotesque body. Here, then, the freak show means something new: the new freak show is a performative embodiment of the grotesque, *an act of collision within a body*, a self-made freakishness.

Embodying many of the elements of Bakhtin's grotesque body, Manson's video for "The Beautiful People" is a testament to Manson's place in the heavy metal carnival of the grotesque. The video is described by *The Times* as being filled with "creepy-crawly, Tim-Burton-gone-wrong, dirt-freak imagery" (Preira). While many of the images Bakhtin describes in his discussion of the grotesque are not explicitly seen, many are suggested through metaphoric imagery. In the video, the band performs in what appears to be an old classroom, cluttered with prostheses

**Fig. 6.1**    Marilyn Manson, "The Beautiful People" (Sigismondi 1996)

and medical and laboratory equipment. During the video, we see Manson performing on stilts and wearing a gown-length outfit, goggles, and a bald cap. Throughout, he wears other costumes such as a corset, a straightjacket, neck and head braces (see Fig. 6.1), an antiquated dental instrument in his mouth, and a black leather pilot's cap. The other four band members appear sporadically throughout the video. One guitarist is costumed in a leather outfit reminiscent of Edward Scissorhands, the bassist wears his staple baby doll dress and fishnets, the drummer appears to be wearing an unlaced straight jacket, and the other guitarist wears a plain gray suit with aviator goggles. They are all heavily made up and their movements are jerky and mechanical. Though many images appear quickly and it is sometimes unclear what you are looking at, recognizable images include dental x-rays, medical instruments in jars, worms, mannequin heads, plastic hands which are made to look as though they are saluting, two bald women dancing gracefully on stilts, a fat man in his underwear, marching boots, mannequins with prosthetic legs, and a man walking with a prosthetic leg. Manson's body is freaked both by his costumes and the surrounding scenery. Being the lead singer in the video gives him power but also ownership of the visual story the video tells. His body is thus marked by images that evoke the freak body because of their relation to disabled and grotesque bodies.

The mix of beautiful and ugly, feminine and masculine, old and young, earthly and fantastic, weak and strong, suggests an alignment that is made explicit in the song's lyrics: "the beautiful people ... the horrible people" (Marilyn Manson 1996). The frequent appearance of medical and dental equipment paired with the video's filthy and dark images captures Bakhtin's notion that the grotesque is a collision of inside and outside. Similarly, reflecting Arturo's ideas of the freak body in *Geek Love*, Manson sings "Hey you, what do you see? /Something beautiful? Something free?" (Marilyn Manson 1996). For both Arturo and Manson, the grotesque body is both ruined and beautiful and ultimately a path to freedom. The carnival and the freak body are both grotesque and beautiful, as full of contradictions as Manson himself. Manson illustrates that contact with the freak body is not the fearful encounter it used to be, as in the horror film, but a desirable mixing of bodies in order to create something new, the self-made freak. His appreciation of the freak of nature seems to suggest that contact with the freak body is not limited in its desirability to the made freak, but rather that the made freak is a move toward the born freak body.

His video for the song "mOBSCENE," makes this point more directly. The clip opens with Manson on stilts dressed as a circus ringmaster as he walks down a dirt road followed by an elephant and two female performers. The black and white clip, which is a clear nod to the traditional traveling circus, gives way to a full-color close-up of a more modern and much darker Manson ringmaster as the song begins. This seems to signify a new freak show celebrating self-made freaks.

Many of the images seen throughout the video suggest this new freak show. Rather than conjoined twins, for instance, two young women appear corseted together back-to-back (see Fig. 6.2). In another scene, a woman wearing only her underwear is reflected in a funhouse mirror. The way that her body is distorted and its image duplicated makes it appear as though there is flesh joining multiple women together. This illusion, as well as the corseted women, present the appearance of being conjoined but, in the new freak show, theirs is a false and temporary

**Fig. 6.2**   "Conjoined Twins," "mOBSCENE" (Manson and Kloss 2003)

impairment. Similarly, the prosthetic legs shown in the video are an interesting comment on the loss of the more traditional sideshow freak. It is because of medical advances such as these prostheses that freaks of nature disappeared from the freak show. Their place here speaks to that loss but also celebrates the advances that have allowed those with disabilities to escape the title of freak. In other words, it heralds a new freak show but also—by glorifying medical equipment and prosthetics, as in "The Beautiful People"—celebrates the loss of the old one.

Another of the video's characters, a woman with her head in a birdcage, certainly calls to mind the pinheads of the traditional freak shows (see Fig. 6.3). She appears childish because of her dress and pigtails but is clearly a grown woman. Her caged head suggests an imprisoned mind, reflecting the portrayal of pinheads as childlike and imbecilic. In a later scene, the same girl is shown only now she holds a white peacock, changing the image's context. Clearly the bird is shown to remind us that *it* belongs in the cage—not the girl. Placing the woman in the cage suggests that she is an animal, a nod perhaps to the freak show's tendency for creating hybrid human/animal exhibits. However, the girl couldn't look less like an animal and thus foregrounds the inhumanity of the traditional freak show. In other words, she is no more animal than the freaks who were exhibited as animalistic (Grace McDaniels, "The

**Fig. 6.3**  Women of "mOBSCENE" (Manson and Kloss 2003)

Mule-Faced Woman" or Jo-Jo, "The Dog-Faced Boy," for example) and often treated as such. Certainly the new freak show, where the freaks have chosen their otherness, is less problematic in this way.

There are two other interesting freak bodies in the video. The first is a child whose head and arms are bandaged suggesting a burn or some other type of injury (see Fig. 6.3). The extent of the girl's injury would not be too severe; bandages are used to help heal temporary injuries. The other is an obese woman in underwear and a pearl necklace (again, see Fig. 6.3). She is heavily made up and dances provocatively in a way that marks her as sexual. Interestingly, in one of the video's final scenes, these two appear in the same frame as the birdcage girl, only now the bandaged child holds Manson's decapitated head in her arms. She appears playful, as if she is holding a doll instead of a head, while the other two women stand to either side of her. The head held by the bandaged girl inverts the idea that a child with a disability is endearing while adults with similar limitations are not. Here the child appears simultaneously innocent and scary, while the two adult women who flank her are normalized or neutralized in comparison.

**Fig. 6.4**   Manson and high-heeled legs, "mOBSCENE" (Manson and Kloss 2003)

Finally, it is significant that while all of the bodies in the video are freakish, only the female bodies are disabled or impaired: the contorted body in the funhouse mirror, the faux Siamese twins, the birdcage girl, the fat woman, the bandaged child, and the zombie dancers. Even the prosthetic legs are wearing high heels (see Fig. 6.4). Male bodies include Manson himself, his band, and male soldiers, and all appear able-bodied. The video traffics in female grotesqueness and aligns disability with femininity and weakness. This alignment suggests an unwillingness to align masculinity and disability, implying that it is acceptable to objectify a disabled or freakish female body while disabled men are better left out of view. While this is certainly not a unique view of gender or disability, it is contradictory that Manson, who seems, at times, to reject traditional views of masculinity, would make such a connection. It is these small moments that suggest that it is Manson's aggressive maleness that makes his freakish body even more subversive.

In his autobiography, Manson discusses a few of his personal experiences with people with disabilities, most notably his association with a deaf female groupie named Alyssa. He recalls that the band had met her at the perfect time because Pogo, the band's keyboard player, had recently told them that he fantasized about having sex with a deaf girl because "he could say whatever he wanted without upsetting her or feeling embarrassed" (*The Long Hard Road Out of Hell* 201). Manson describes how the band covered Alyssa with various meat products, urinated on her, and filmed her. The band "decided that Pogo should get to live out his fantasy" and the band watched as he had sex with her "from behind, which was appropriate because she has a dog leash on at the time and he was holding the leash." In addition to the many obscenities Pogo shouted at her during the act, he yelled "I'm going to come in your useless ear canal." Though he admits it was "maybe one of the darkest things we had ever heard," Manson defends the act, saying that "I do not feel like she was being exploited by any means because ... she was very excited to be a part of it [and] found it to be art and was having a good time" (202–203). Alyssa's female body is made a freak body not because of her deafness, but because of the way her body is made grotesque and pornographic, and is exhibited by the male viewer.

Manson's argument that Alyssa was willing and therefore not exploited reflects the morality arguments people once had about freak show exhibits. However, his point does not consider that just because she was willing to be debased does not mean that the male band members were not exploiting her; and certainly Manson's retelling of this story for his book is exploitative in that its shock factor helps build his image. The retelling of this incident, and of course the incident itself, is not merely misogynistic; Manson tells numerous stories throughout his book that confirm his penchant for mistreating women. This story is different because, while it is given its own short chapter, it does not connect to or serve any purpose in the larger narrative. Because Alyssa is disabled, and because Pogo degrades her during a sexually dominating act, the story seems to promote the idea that disabled women are worthless aside from being objects of sexual pleasure, abuse, or personal entertainment.

While Manson often utilizes images of freakish bodies in positive and forward-thinking ways, he undoes much of that with his handling of an actual disabled person. He illustrates, here and in his videos, that the new freak show has little to do with disability, that the freak of culture is the new freak show. One thing that hasn't changed is the perpetuation of disabled women as doubly negative. Manson's positioning of men as able-bodied, strong, and sexually potent, and women as disabled, weak, and sexually submissive reveals that his concept of the new freak show is one in which patriarchy and the freak of culture are valued.

## "I'M A FREAK BITCH, BABY": THE PERFORMATIVE BODY OF MOTHER MONSTER

Though they have much in common, Lady Gaga is, in many ways, Marilyn Manson's female antithesis: a nurturing mother and teacher, never too controversial, just shocking enough to surprise and interest people but rarely crossing lines that would offend mainstream America. While Gaga similarly embodies the carnivalesque and the grotesque, she does not do so in the same vein; she only has access to the freak body through her subversive femininity. Lady Gaga has also embraced actual images of disability in her performances and costumes and, as with Manson, these read as being inauthentic. Unlike Manson, on the other hand, Gaga's conception of the new freak show seems to esteem both the freak of nature and the freak of culture, and inhabits gender identity as a means to freakishness.

Lady Gaga (born Stefani Germanotta) rose to prominence with the release of her debut album *The Fame* (2008), which boasts more than 15 million worldwide album sales, six Grammy nominations, and 13 MTV Video Music Award nominations ("Lady Gaga Bio"). Her second album, *The Fame Monster* (2009) and its follow up, *Born This* Way (2011), have received similar accolades. She is the only artist of the digital age to break the five million sales mark with her first two singles. Her videos have been viewed online well over one billion times, and she is one of the most popular living celebrities on Facebook, Instagram, and Twitter.[5] Lady Gaga was America's most Googled celebrity of 2009, and was in the top three in both 2010 and 2011 (though somewhat surprisingly she has not shown up on any of Google's yearly *zeitgeist* lists since then) (*Google Zeitgeist*).

Like Manson, Gaga is known for her wild clothing choices, music videos, and performances much more than for her music. She has her own creative team, the Haus of Gaga, who design and create most of her clothes, hairstyles, and the mise-en-scene surrounding her. Some of her most infamous costumes include a bow made out of human hair, lobster claw gloves, a dress made of Kermit the Frog dolls, a meat dress, a bubble dress, soda can hair curlers, lace masks, and a transparent plastic dress

---

[5] As of March 2014, Gaga was the most followed person on Twitter with over 41 million followers.

with white tape crossed over her nipples and a nun's headdress. Also like Manson, her videos and performances have been wildly eclectic; they often blur binaries between male and female, life and death, beauty and ugliness, animal and human, and ability and disability.

A nod to Gaga's perpetual ability to create and recreate representations of hybrid bodies, the *New York Times* has described her as a "real-time version of Photoshop" ("The Year in Style: Lady Gaga"). Such a metaphor is quite apt in characterizing Gaga because, though Photoshop and Gaga were born in the mid-1980s, they are undoubtedly twenty-first century phenomena. Like a Photoshop creation, Gaga's body is constantly subject to reinvention and improvement; both suggest a crisis of authenticity. Her everyday comings and goings have become real-time performance pieces, caught by the media and immediately uploaded onto social media sites with a speed that can lead to the impression that Gaga's look and body are apt to change almost instantly.

That Gaga is a product of her time is essential in understanding her fame and significance in popular culture. Digital celebrity culture can be instantly accessed by the masses through the means of Twitter, Facebook, Instagram, Vine, and other social networking sites and comment boards. Calling her the "first hypermodern pop star," Corona notes that Gaga's "unique spectacle" speaks to the "the hypermodern pace of cultural consumption" (13, 12). She argues that Gaga's "elaborate performances and sartorial experimentation are deployed to create visual impressions that are practically tailor-made for the age of viral marketing and generate expectations of ever grander spectacles" (1–2). The accessibility that fans have to Gaga—and she to them—has both made and kept her famous. Though technology has aided in the creation of celebrity for at least half a century, the instantaneity of today's media has allowed Gaga to react to changing social trends immediately as well as have open access to her fans, much like Manson.

Because she associates herself with freakishness, this availability would suggest that, like the freak show, people would get bored at seeing so much Gaga so often. However, because every time we see her she looks so different, she doesn't seem as overexposed as she actually is. Her perpetual transformability, both through costuming and endless media representations, links her to Bakhtin's carnival which is marked by its impermanence and refusal to stop changing. David Annandale takes this notion further, arguing that Bakhtin's carnival, "by virtue of being contained within a limited space and time," has been criticized as being "little more than a social safety valve," something that would help people blow off steam and then allow a return to the "status quo." However, because "Lady Gaga's carnival is unending" (she is Gaga on stage but also at the gym, the grocery store, and so on), she is able to transcend the carnival and can truly be transgressive (143). Gaga's excess and inability to stop "performing Gaga" even in mundane locals such as the grocery store allows her to affect rather than help to maintain the status quo.

Because Gaga's fame is so deeply embedded in today's viral communities and because she grew up Manhattan's affluent Upper West Side in a two-parent Caucasian household, questions about Gaga's authenticity have surrounded her fame.[6] As Burton notes, "Where many artists have introduced the abject into their works to discuss the crisis of subjectivity as a challenge to the body politic … Gaga operates within, and is legitimized by, those cultural institutions that have been fundamental in reifying notions of the unified subject" (3). Her abject spectacle does not come from a place of transgression, but rather operates from within cultural institutions that have helped shape the very notions she claims to fight against. As Elizabeth Kate Switaj notes, "Gaga-the-performance-artist challenges the systems of power through which Gaga-the-pop-star benefits" (34). For example, Gaga speaks for inclusion and acceptance of all people but does so from a position of privilege; this is seen in many images from music videos and photo shoots in which Gaga's thin, able-bodied, white, female form is purposefully highlighted against the bodies of non-white, disabled, and otherwise othered bodies.

For Gaga, her feeling of being an outcast in high school (an experience nearly every American teenager relates to, to some degree) is enough to gain entrance into a position of otherness. Burton argues that

Lady Gaga demonstrates what Deborah Caslav Covino calls a "shared abjection"; one that is "grounded in concern for the body of the Other" in a bid to generate "a method for reenvisioning gendered social, political and sexual relations, as well as providing a critical approach to other forms of exclusion." And … what is significant is that from her position of centrality and privilege, she affects a carnivalesque resistance to the symbolic order that celebrates difference. (2)

---

[6]Camille Paglia even tells us that Gaga "attended the same upscale Manhattan private school as Paris and Nicky Hilton" (Paglia).

The central way in which Gaga demonstrates a shared abjection is through her persona as "Mother Monster." Though Gaga spent some time appearing as her male alter-ego, Jo Calderone, and has consistently blurred male and female imagery in her videos and performances, she undoubtedly identifies as a female, as both of her stage names—*Lady* Gaga and *Mother* Monster—attest to.[7] However, Gaga may be more subversive in embracing her femininity, as the pairing of motherhood and monstrosity suggests, than she is in her failed attempts at gender-bending. As she says in "Bad Romance" (Lady Gaga 2009) and "Born This Way" (Lady Gaga 2011), she is "freak bitch"—her freakishness is found, in other words, in her abject representation of the female body.[8]

By embracing her role as mother, Gaga is entering into the position of other through the only means available to her: womanhood. Hers is not a patriarchal womanhood, nor an entirely liberated one. Her "manifesto" at the opening of her "Born This Way" video provides some insight: "a birth of magnificent and magical proportions took place. But the birth was not finite; it was infinite ... as the eternal mother hovered in the multiverse, another more terrifying birth took place: the birth of evil" (Lady Gaga 2011).[9] The manifesto, which celebrates the grotesquery of childbirth as a continual process, brings the maternal body into the realm of the monstrous grotesque (see Fig. 6.5). By embodying the concept of the monstrous feminine, Gaga "revitalizes the etymological foundations of the term *monster*; that is, she shows, reveals, demonstrates all that is abjected or exiled to the margins as it relates to maternal subjectivity" (Burton 2). Highlighting the in-betweenness of the othered body, Gaga is both monstrous and female in a way that is carnivalesque in its simultaneous absurdity and subversion. The video's imagery suggests the infinite wombs and births mentioned in the manifesto, but this overly theatrical prelude to the song contrasts with the rest of the video. Once the song itself begins, we get a stripped down Gaga—no costumes, very little makeup, only in her underwear—dancing along to a pop beat reminiscent of Madonna's "Express Yourself." The absurdity

---

[7] Ironically, the night Gaga premiered Jo Calderone, the 2011 MTV Video Music Awards, was the same night she won the award for best female video.

[8] In "Dance in the Dark" (Lady Gaga 2009) she similarly says that she is a "free bitch," an oxymoronic description that implies freedom despite her position as female.

[9] For full lyrics see: http://ladygaga.wikia.com/wiki/Manifesto_of_Mother_Monster.

**Fig. 6.5**    "Birth scene," "Born This Way" (Knight 2011)

of such a contrast underscores the point Gaga seems to be making here and throughout the video: that Gaga—and by suggestion her Little Monsters—are both beautiful and ugly, old and young, regal and pedestrian, singular and plural, weak and powerful, good and evil.

This is also implied by the appearance of Zombie Boy in the "Born This Way" video. Rick Genest, aka Zombie Boy, is famous for his full body tattoo that makes him resemble a living corpse. Genest claims that he will "challenge your sensibilities about what you believe to be beautiful" ("My Story"). In the video, he mostly stands scowling at the camera while Gaga, who is painted and costumed to look like his twin sister, dances with and around him (see Fig. 6.6). Though a contrast is certainly made here—she is animated and happy while he appears dark and lifeless—the contrast would have been more easily achieved if Gaga had not appeared in zombie makeup but barefaced. Instead, Zombie Boy's cameo merely highlights the difference between Gaga and a more authentic made freak. Her freakishness is temporary—after the shoot, she washes the makeup off—while Zombie Boy is permanently committed to his role as freak. This speaks to a social hierarchy within the freak world

**Fig. 6.6**   Lady Gaga and Zombie Boy in "Born This Way" (Knight 2011)

that existed in the freak show as well. The born freak acts were on the top because of their authenticity and rarity, while novelty acts and made freaks were considered to have lower status. In the case of the self-made freak, the permanence of Zombie Boy's freak status trumps Gaga's even though they are both freaks of culture. She can take off the many costumes she wears but because her freakishness is impermanent, next to him she appears to be a poser. She therefore seems to be less of a freak while his monstrosity is underscored by her posing as his match; he is the manifestation of her vision. As Corona points out: "In popular culture as a whole, the blending of the beautiful with the monstrous is a well-established motif. The contrast of beast and beauty is used to provoke a reckoning with prevailing ideals of appearance, tolerance, justice, and sexuality" (8–9).

Since the inception of her fame, Gaga has used the monstrous feminine in order to relay a sustained message of acceptance, and performs through the "carnivalized character" of Mother Monster in order to resist "the homogenizing force of the body politic" (Burton 6). Betcher points out that Gaga's use of the body as a vehicle for expressing "pain, anger, fear, disease, and decay [as well as] the carnal and the corpse [and] the conclusiveness of mortality" has been a staple of the male-dominated heavy metal music scene with artists such as Marilyn Manson and Alice Cooper (114). However, Gaga's pairing of the abject with the distinctly feminine makes hers a specifically gendered statement, whereas similar male representations like Manson and Cooper's tend to be ambiguously gendered. Her femininity is not, however, an innocuous one. As Corona points out, Gaga came onto the music scene having been "already defiled" unlike many of her pop predecessors, such as Britney Spears, the state of whose virginity was public knowledge (9). For Gaga, being female means embracing her sexual identity and pushing the limits of what is expected of female pop artists. Her monstrosity, then, is not simply in being female, but in being an excessive, unrestrained, and monstrous female.

Like her identity as "mother," Gaga's use of the "monster" identity seems to have multiple contexts for her. She has said that "[c]elebrity life and media culture are probably the most overbearing pop-cultural conditions that we as young people have to deal with, because it forces us to judge ourselves. I guess what I am trying to do is take the monster and turn the monster into a fairy tale" (Corona qt. Lady Gaga 8). Here, the monster is both fame itself and the products of her fame, her Little Monsters. Her aim is to alchemize the damaging internalizations of pop culture into a more positive sense of self for her fans. However, elsewhere, Gaga has said:

> Each one of these songs on my album represents a different demon that I've faced in myself, so the music is much more personal. I don't write about fame or money at all on this new record. So we talked about monsters and how, I believe, that innately we're all born with the monsters already inside of us—I guess in Christianity they call it original sin—the prospect that we will, at some point, sin in our lives, and we will, at some point, have to face our own demons, and they're already inside of us. (Corona qt. Lady Gaga 8)

Here, Gaga uses the concept of "monster" as justification for her freak identity: she is no longer writing about fame but about how she is monstrous like her fans. She also points to the Judeo-Christian notion of the Fall, claiming that we are all monsters from birth. Monstrosity, then, is not a modern affliction as she suggests in the first quote, but something innate and inescapable in each of us. Gaga is pointing out how, as with viewers of disability porn, we as spectators are already freaks.

The strength of this concept in Gaga's performance is that it works to attract other self-identifying "freaks of culture" or cultural outcasts, "an effort that Gaga hopes will ultimately empower them to express the 'monster' within them" (Corona 11). However, Gaga does not seem aware of her failure to take into consideration the connection between the disabled body and the way she uses the concept of monstrosity. Long considered monsters or monstrous births, people with physical disabilities seem to be excluded from Gaga's rationale. If we apply the above quote to those with monstrous bodies, then Gaga seems to be implying either that we all have the potential to become monstrous through fate or accident, or, a much more conservatively critical interpretation, that disability is somehow connected to original sin. Gaga's brand of performativity essentially ignores the history of the monstrous body or is unaware of it, unlike Manson who acknowledges the past and then celebrates moving away from it.

For Gaga, monstrosity is new and can be made new again and again. The positivity of the monstrous, for Gaga, is that it reflects the perpetual invention of identity, the in-betweenness of identity, and a lack of clearly defined boundaries or an unending ambiguity that is characteristic of celebrity and the media age and thus Gaga herself. The state of monstrosity is "a position expressed throughout her performances, music and in her daily fashion transitions where tropes of the grotesque, the freak and the monstrous are reasserted and simultaneously destroyed, allowing new territories for subjects to find and be validated in their own forms of representation" (Burton 2). Because it is changeable, monstrosity is freeing; it is an opportunity for new modes of expression. It is her femininity that makes her a "freak bitch" and this monstrosity that makes her a "free bitch."

We see a convoluted representation of the monster body in Gaga's portrayals of disability. Gaga has spoken out as part of the fight for disability rights, claiming to have changed the lives of her disabled fans.[10] Her appropriation of disability as a prop or a cultural statement, however, is more troublesome than any of Gaga's other controversies. This is perhaps because she has used disability in her photos, music videos, and shows so often, or maybe because disability is a sensitive subject that tends to make people feel uncomfortable. One example of such an

---

[10] "I had girls in wheelchairs crying to me at meet-and-greets, telling me that when they saw [the "Bad Romance"] video it changed their lives" (Robinson).

appropriation is found in a series of photos from her "Superdeluxe" edition of *The Fame Monster* in which Gaga appears disabled. In one photo, she uses metal crutches and in another she appears to have fallen out of a diamond encrusted wheelchair. Another example is the 2009 MTV Video Music Awards where Gaga performed her hit song "Paparazzi" while using a metal crutch as a prop. Halfway through the performance a woman in a wheelchair was rolled onstage where she sat and danced.[11] The intention behind the woman's presence onstage is unclear. At the end of the performance, fake blood began pooling around Gaga's abdomen as she was lifted into the air.

The performance that has probably garnered the most attention took place in July 2011. While performing in Australia, Gaga rolled onto the stage to sing her hit "You and I" while wearing a mermaid tail and seated in a wheelchair. The performance has been met with conflicting reactions from both the media and disability groups. A spokesperson for the advocacy group Life Rolls On Foundation has said, "I invite her to learn more about the 5.6 million Americans who live with paralysis. They, like me, unfortunately, don't use a wheelchair for shock value" (Heasley). Others had more positive responses such as Stella Young, writer for *Ramp Up,* who says that Gaga's mermaid performance doesn't make any more of a comment on disability than any of her other performances. She cites Gaga's entrance into the Grammys while being carried inside an egg, arguing that it certainly wasn't a comment on chickens. She added that "as wheelchair users we celebrate our chairs in all sorts of ways all the time. If Lady Gaga wants in on that action, more power to her. She did, after all, have quite the mobility issue dressed as a mermaid" (Young). While one can see the logic in Young's point, the problem is twofold. First, that Gaga chose to dress as a mermaid and thus chose to temporarily disable herself is insensitive to those who have not been able to make that choice for themselves. Further, Young reads Gaga's use of the chair as celebratory but does not take into account the implications of such an appropriation. Gaga's use of the chair, in other words, is not

---

[11] It is unknown whether she was actually disabled, though most critics seem to think she isn't.

opening society's eyes about disability rights, nor is it bringing the disabled community into the spotlight in a positive way. It does not send a message of acceptance or tolerance or glamorize disability. If anything, it brings disability into the realm of the theatrical, of the carnivalesque. In doing so, Gaga is not merely making an artistic statement, nor is she simply exploiting disability (to clarify, I don't think Gaga is *intentionally* exploiting anyone). As Bakhtin notes, the heart of carnival culture is neither merely art nor spectacle but rather "[i]t belongs to the borderline between art and life" (7). Gaga uses disability to bring the gap between art and life: for her, they are interchangeable.

Hebdige has argued that subcultural expressions are "always mediated: inflected by the historical context in which [they are] encountered; posited upon a specific ideological field which gives it particular life and particular meanings" (80). Thus, there is a significant difference between the egg in which Gaga was carried into the Grammy Awards and the wheelchairs and crutches she and her dancers have used on stage. The egg simply does not have the same real-life significance that a wheelchair does. Similarly, when Manson utilizes crutches and other medical devices in his performances, the cultural context is different because although these objects reference sickness and disability, they suggest transitory conditions that are common in people's lives. Gaga's repeated use of the wheelchair as a prop, on the other hand, bridges the gap between art and life in a way that is more culturally loaded because the chair suggests a more permanent—and frightening—disability.

Lady Gaga's music video for her song "Paparazzi" has a clearly negative view of the disabled body. The clip, presented more as a short film than a music video, opens with Gaga and her boyfriend, played by Alexander Skarsgård, in bed together. The pair move on to a balcony where they have a fight when the boyfriend becomes distracted by the paparazzi filming them and throws Gaga over the ledge. After watching her fall to the pavement below, photographers gather around to capture the spectacle of her lying on the ground. Newspapers and magazines swirl toward the camera with headlines reading "Lady No More Gaga?" "Lady Gaga is Over," and "Gaga Hits Rock Bottom." The song finally begins as Gaga pulls up in front of her mansion in a limousine. Her dancers lift her out of the car, place her in a wheelchair, and strip her down into a gold metal bodysuit. She wears a matching neck brace and helmet and holds metal crutches. These symbols are used to indicate both the destruction of Gaga's body and the demise of her fame. She

**Fig. 6.7**   Lady Gaga with crutches, "Paparazzi" (Åkerlund 2009)

rises from her chair and begins to dance around in a way that is especially awkward next to her able-bodied dancers. This scene is contrasted with cut-in images of a non-disabled and black leather clad Gaga thrashing around on a couch in a sexual way. Toward the video's end, a fully healed Gaga takes revenge on her boyfriend—who now inexplicably wears an eye patch—poisoning him for disabling her. Now the headlines read: "Gaga: the New It Girl," "She's Back," and "We Love Her Again."

The commentary is clear: being disabled is akin to weakness and failure. Gaga is only able to succeed—in both her fame and in enacting revenge on her boyfriend—when her able-bodiedness is restored. It is important to note that there is no hint about how she recovers from her disability. That her boyfriend is disabled at the end of the video speaks to his weakness as well; it is only once he is injured and thus emasculated that Gaga kills him. The portrayal of disability as a temporary state perpetuates the medical model of disability (that a disabled person is just waiting to be cured or corrected). The impermanence of her disability is evident symbolism intended to tell the clichéd story of a woman overcoming adversity. In other words, disability is not something to fear because it can be fixed or overcome. It can be argued that Gaga is trying to problematize common perceptions of normality. However, she does not seem to be attempting to make disability normal. This is especially so because we see Gaga both disabled and able-bodied in the same video. The disabled Gaga is awkward, desexualized, and unattractive. Her dancers do not look at her and the viewer shares the feeling of wanting to look elsewhere (see Fig. 6.7). The non-disabled Gaga, on the other hand, is fabulous, sexy, and interesting. She is flanked by men who want and adore her. Other characters in the video look at her. The video certainly makes a comment on the ways we look—or don't look—at spectacle and how the disabled body is viewed in public and private spaces. In the scenes in which Gaga is temporarily disabled, she is hidden from the cameras by giant sunglasses and quickly wheeled inside the privacy of her mansion, essentially hidden from the public's gaze. She recovers in the private space of her home, a process we do not see ("The Transcontinental Disability Choir"). The public/private split seems to reinforce shameful stigmas about disability, that it is embarrassing, should be hidden from view, or should be dealt with quietly.

Ultimately, Gaga's sense of the new freak show is hybridized. She embraces the freak show with its connection to the carnivalesque grotesque, but because hers is an appropriated freakishness, she must reimagine the freak show as something that can be equalized across different levels of freakishness. She becomes a freak body when she is Mother Monster, but, like Manson, fails to appropriate freakishness meaningfully when she comes in contact with the true freak body or representations of it. Gaga seems to be suggesting that it is in embodying social norms about heterosexuality and gender identities that one accesses freakishness.

# Conclusion: Spooky Kids & Little Monsters: Disseminating the Freak Show

Since the apex of his fame, tenacious rumors have followed Manson around: such as one that claims he played Paul Pfeiffer on *The Wonder Years*, or another alleging that he had his lower ribs removed so that he could perform fellatio on himself. Lady Gaga has been the subject of similar rumors, most notably that she is actually a man or a hermaphrodite. Ann Torrusio says that "[t]he perverse desire for the public to label Gaga as abnormal or malformed is not unlike the rumors that circulated about Marilyn Monroe having six toes on one foot … It is as if an ogling public feels compelled to conjure up freakish physical attributes to stars they find especially compelling, perhaps in an attempt to categorize them as 'not like us'" (162). More so, I believe such rumors, in regard to celebrities like Monroe, Manson, and Gaga, speak to the viewing public's need for authentication. In other words, people seek both a confirmation of and an explanation for an otherwise unexplainable freakishness. Manson and Gaga make viewers uneasy in their assumed freakishness, thus we look for ways to freak them more permanently and authentically. In other words, the viewer wants to make the freak of culture a freak of nature. Here, the spectator helps to create a projection of freakishness that is not otherwise visible or tangible. In the cases of Manson and Gaga, this image-forming has been widespread and has had a fairly significant impact on the way the viewing public, and non-fans in particular, read the two stars. The viewers' interaction with the creation of freakishness is significant as it suggests a direct interplay that has not yet been overtly present in the representations of freakishness I have explored.

J.L. Williams, *Media, Performative Identity, and the New American Freak Show*, DOI 10.1007/978-3-319-66462-0

Manson and Gaga have created a perpetual freakishness that is made new again and again. For both, there is no difference between their created identity and their behind-the-scenes personas. Elizabeth Barfoot Christian suggests that Gaga is the personification of "Baudrillard's theory of simulacra and simulation, where the image has replaced the original," a notion that holds true for Manson as well (Turner qt. Christian 190). Both have made statements that suggest that they are simultaneously always and never performing, such as Manson's statement that "I'm completely unlike a lot of other performers ... because they tell everyone their performance is 'just a show' ... It's not just a show for me. It's my life. I live my art" (Wiedorhorn qt. Manson), and Gaga's claim that she isn't a "character or a persona" but that she is "always Lady Gaga," someone whose "art is not a mask [but] is her life" (Murfett qt. Gaga and Turner qt. Strauss 191). On the other hand, both also speak to the idea that their identities are lies. Manson has said that he chose the stage name Marilyn Manson, "the fakest stage name of all," because "it is to say that this is what show business is, fake." He explains, "Marilyn Monroe wasn't even her real name, Charles Manson isn't his real name, and now, I'm taking that to be my real name, but what's real? You can't find the truth [so] you just pick the lie you like the best" (*Marilyn Manson Wiki*). Similarly, Gaga has said that she wants to "fight so hard for [the idea of being Gaga] every day that the lie becomes the truth" (Turner qt. Gaga 190–191).

The meaning of such intentional, perpetual performativity must be understood as a "visible construction, a loaded choice" that "directs attention to itself [and] gives itself to be read" (Hebdige 101). That such spectacle is obviously inauthentic to some degree is, according to Hebdige, essential in its definition as subcultural and subversive. Such culturally coded performances must be fabricated, they must "display their own codes ... or at least demonstrate that codes are there to be used and abused" (101–102). It is clear that these codes have been received and internalized by the viewer. This is not only seen in fans' devout dedication to the artists, but also in their appropriations of the artists' imagery, and their self-prescribed labels as Little Monsters, Spooky Kids, and freaks.

Manson and Gaga have had a significant give and take with their fans in other ways as well. Manson and his fans have a huge presence on the internet to this day, though Manson's online presence has declined since the 1990s. At the height of his fame, Manson had an enormous amount of direct contact with his fans including personally written newsletters, journals, and blogs, webcasts, podcasts, and fan conferences. Gaga has an even more significant interaction with her fans, championing causes that are important to her fan base such as LGBTQ causes and AIDS relief; creating a social networking website for her "super fans," littlemonsters. com, on which Gaga herself often posts; giving her manager's personal email address to her Little Monsters; and taking suggestions from fans on everything from Gaga's hair color and costuming to set lists and concert lighting (Pearson). She has also developed her own foundation, called the Born This Way Foundation, whose mission is to create "a safe community that helps connect young people with the skills and opportunities they need to build a kinder, braver world" ("Our Mission"). One of the foundations newest features includes the Born This Way bus in which her fans can receive professional mental health counseling at her concerts. Both artists' fans have renamed themselves in homage to their idols (Manson's Spooky Kids and Gaga's Little Monsters[1]) and both Manson and Gaga fans are known for appropriating similar ways of dressing themselves (see Fig. A.1).

It is the interaction between performer and viewer as well as the blurring of the authentic and inauthentic freak identity that allows fans to connect so strongly with these artists and others like them. That Manson and Gaga are not born freaks allows them a normalcy that cannot be completely hidden with costumes, imitations of disability, or even the self-label of freak. Buying into freak culture, rather than being born into it, is a choice for many that allows them to mark themselves as separate from society as well as simultaneously buy into a society that accepts them. Freakishness is commodified, then, but it is also disseminated. Because Manson and Gaga bridge the gap between authentic and inauthentic, mainstream and fringe, freak and norm, comedic and tragic, performance and real life, and, most importantly, perhaps, performer and viewer, they underscore Bakhtin's notion that carnival—and by extension the freak show—makes no distinction between performers and viewers. As Bakhtin attests: "Carnival is not a spectacle seen by the people; they live in it, and everyone participates because its very idea embraces all the people. While carnival lasts, there is no other life outside it" (7).

---

[1] It is unclear how predominantly the label of Spooky Kids still persists in the Manson fan base though it seems to have declined in popularity since the mid-1990s.

**Fig. A.1**   16-year-old Manson fan and author of this book (1998)

Thus, if the entertainment we consume attempts to appropriate the cultural work of the freak show—as the horror, reality television, documentary, pornography, music culture, and live performances that I've explored do—then carnival is everlasting and ever-present, and if we are perpetually in carnival then we are also continually apart from and a part of carnival. The freak has never stopped looking back, despite the distances media have put between the freak and viewer, but the power behind that look has been shifting. It could be said that the freak, once powerless, now has a tremendous power over the viewing public who continue to look and see themselves reflected back more than ever.

# FILMOGRAPHY

*The Bone Collector*, 1999.
*Candyman*, 1992.
*Dracula* , 1931.
*The Elephant Man*, 1980.
*Flesh and Blood*, 2007.
*Freaks*, 1932.
*Friday the Thirteenth*, 1980.
*Frankenstein* , 1931.
*The Funhouse*, 1981.
*The Horse Whisperer*, 1998.
*The Hunchback of Notre Dame* , 1923.
*The Man Without a Face*, 1993.
*The Miracle Worker.* 1962.
*The Mummy* , 1932.
*Murderball*, 2005.
*My Left Foot*, 1989.
*The Phantom of the Opera* , 1925.
*The Pride of the Yankees.* 1942.
*Psycho* , 1960.
*Rosemary's Baby*, 1968.
*Sick: The Life and Death of Bob Flanagan Supermasochist*, 1997.

© The Editor(s) (if applicable) and The Author(s) 2017      173
J.L. Williams, *Media, Performative Identity, and the New American
Freak Show*, DOI 10.1007/978-3-319-66462-0

*Sideshow: Alive on the Inside!*, 1996.
*Snuff*, 1976
*The Texas Chainsaw Massacre*, 1974.
*Tiptoes*. 2003.

# REFERENCES

*A Brief History of the Carte de Visite*. n.d. 17 February 2012. http://www.photographymuseum.com/histsw.htm.

Accordino, Michael, Robert L. Hewes and Jeanmarie Crimoli. "Public Perceptions of People with Disabilities." *Psychology of Disability*. Ed. Joseph F. Stano. Linn Creek: Aspen Professional Services, 2009.

Adams, Rachel. *Sideshow U.S.A*. Chicago: University of Chicago Press, 2001.

Adams, Tiphany (@tiphanyadams). "I choose to take on my own challenges... DAILY! #SWEAT http://instagr.am/p/RS3nmjneDT/." Twitter.com. 27 October 2012, 12:53 p.m. 29 October 2012.

Allen, James, et. al. *Without Sanctuary: Lynching Photography in America*. Santa Fe: Twin Palms, 2000.

"Amputee Sex." *Porn Hub*. 16 May 2017. https://www.pornhub.com/view_video.php?viewkey=ph58c9960b16c1f.

"Amputee Sucking." *Porn Hub*. 16 May 2017. https://www.pornhub.com/view_video.php?viewkey=ph58adab3131199.

Angel, Auti (@autiangel). "@Lagute @angelarockwood @tiphanyadams AWE THANKS!!! Getting ready to watch in LA. And you're beautiful just the way you are!" Twitter.com. 9 October 2012, 3: 24 p.m. 29 October 2012.

Annandale, David. "Rabelais Meets Vogue: the Construction of Carnival, Beauty and Grotesque." *The Performance Identities of Lady Gaga*. Ed. Richard J. Gray II. Jefferson: McFarland & Co., 2012. 142–159.

Auslander, Philip. *Liveness, Performance in a Mediatized Culture*. London: Routledge, 1999.

Baddeley, Gavin. *Dissecting Marilyn Manson*. London: Plexus, 2005.

Bakhtin, Mikhail. *Rabelais and His World*. Trns. Helene Iswolsky. Bloomington: Indiana UP, 1984.

© The Editor(s) (if applicable) and The Author(s) 2017
J.L. Williams, *Media, Performative Identity, and the New American Freak Show*, DOI 10.1007/978-3-319-66462-0

Barounis, Cynthia. "Cripping Heterosexuality, Queering Able-Bodiedness: Murderball, Brokeback Mountain and the Contested Masculine Body." *Journal of Visual Culture*. 8.1 (2009): 54–75. August 2012.

Bazin, André. *What Is Cinema?* Translated by Hugh Gray. Berkeley: University of California Press, 1967.

Betcher, Sharon V. "Becoming Flesh of My Flesh: Feminist and Disability Theologies on the Edge of Posthumanist Discourse." *Journal of Feminist Studies in Religion*. 26.2 (2010): 107–118. *Project Muse*. 22 May 2012.

Bogdan, Robert. *Freak Show: Presenting Human Oddities for Amusement and Profit*. Chicago: The University of Chicago Press, 1988.

Bourdieu, Pierre. "On Television." *Media and Cultural Studies, Key Works*. Revised Edition. Ed. Meenakshi Gigi Durham and Douglas M. Kellner. Oxford: Blackwell, 2006. 328–336.

Burton, Laini. "Abject Appeal and the Monstrous Feminine in Lady Gaga's self-fashioned persona 'Mother Monster.'" *Evil, Women and the Feminine*. May 2012. Prague, Czech Republic. Unpublished conference paper, 2012. *Inter-Disciplinary.Net*. 29 May 2012.

Butler, Judith. *Bodies that Matter*. NY: Routledge, 2011.

Carroll, Noel. *The Philosophy of Horror*. NY: Routledge, 1990.

Caulfield, Keith. "Lady Gaga Scores Second No. 1 Album with 'Artpop.'" *Billboard*. 20 Nov 2013. Mar 2014.

Chandler, Daniel. "'Notes on 'The Gaze.'" 1998. 18 October 2013.

Church, David. "Fantastic Films, Fantastic Bodies: Speculations on the Fantastic and Disability Representation." 31 October 2006. Offscreen.Com. 18 February 2012.

Clover, Carol J. *Men, Women, and Chainsaws*. Princeton: Princeton UP, 1992.

Corona, Victor P. "Memory, Monsters, and Lady Gaga." *Journal of Popular Culture* 44.2 (2012): 1–19.

DeBord, Guy. "The Commodity as Spectacle." *Media and Cultural Studies, Key Works*. Revised Edition. Ed. Meenakshi Gigi Durham and Douglas M. Kellner. Oxford: Blackwell, 2006. 117–121.

DePoy, Elizabeth and Stephen French Gilson. "Looking Back." *Studying Disability*. Los Angeles: Sage, 2011. 9–24.

Dunn, Katherine. *Geek Love*. NY: Vintage, 1989.

Durbach, Nadja. "Monstrosity, Masculinity and Medicine: Re-Examining 'the Elephant Man.'" *Spectacle of Deformity: Freak Shows and Modern British Culture*. Berkeley: University of California Press, 2010. 33–57.

Elman, R. Amy. "Mainstreaming Immobility: Disability Pornography and Its Challenge to Two Movements." *Sourcebook on Violence Against Women*. Sage, 2001. 193–207.

Fahy, Thomas. *Freak Shows and the Modern American Imagination: Constructing the Damaged Body from Willa Cather to Truman Capote*. NY: Palgrave, 2006.

Fetveit, Arild. "Reality in the Digital Era: A paradox in visual culture?" *The Television Studies Reader*. Ed. Robert C. Allen and Annette Hill. London: Routledge, 2004. 543–556.

Fiedler, Leslie. *Freaks: Myths and Images of the Secret Self.* NY: Anchor, 1978.

Fischer, Lucy. "Birth Traumas: Parturition and Horror in 'Rosemary's Baby'." *Cinema Journal* 31.3 (1992): 3–18. Feb 2012.

*Freakshow*. AMC.

"Freaks: Script Synopsis." n.d. *Olga Baclanova*. 2 February 2012.

Friedberg, Anne. *The Virtual Window: From Alberti to Microsoft*. Cambridge: MIT Press, 2006. 18 October 2013.

Fries, Kenny. "Beauty and Variations." *Staring Back: The Disability Experience from the Inside Out*. Ed. Kenny Fries. Plume: New York, 1997. 147–150.

————. "Excavation." *Staring Back: The Disability Experience from the Inside Out*. Ed. Kenny Fries. Plume: New York, 1997. 146.

————. "Introduction." *Staring Back: The Disability Experience from the Inside Out*. Ed. Kenny Fries. Plume: New York, 1997. 1–10.

Garland-Thomson, Rosemarie. *Staring: How We Look*. Oxford: Oxford UP, 2009.

*Google Zeitgeist*. 31 May 2012 and 16 Mar 2014.

Grosz, Elizabeth. "Intolerable Ambiguity: Freaks as/at the Limit." *Freakery: Cultural Spectacles of the Extraordinary Body*. Edited by Rosemarie Garland-Thomson. NY UP, 1996. 55–66.

Grue, Jan. "The problem with inspiration porn: A tentative definition and a provisional critique," *Disability & Society*, vol. 31 no. 6, 838–849.

Hagin, Boaz. "Killed Because of Lousy Ratings: The Hollywood History of Snuff." *The Journal of Popular Film and Television*. 38.1 (January–March 2010): 44–51. *EBSCOhost*. 24 June 2013.

Halnon, Karen Bettez. "Heavy Metal Carnival and Dis-Alienation: The Politics of Grotesque Realism." *Symbolic Interaction*. (2006): 29: 1. 33–48. *JSTOR*. 8 June 2012.

"Handicap Amputee Porn with Half a Leg Screws a Hooker." RawHandicapSex. Com, 16 May 2017. http://members.rawhandicapsex.com/scenes/handicap-amputee-porn-with-half-a-leg-screws-a-hooker-88505.html.

"Harlot Rubs Stumps on Her Tits and Pussy." RawHandicapSex.Com, 16 May 2017. http://members.rawhandicapsex.com/scenes/harlot-rubs-stumps-on-her-tits-and-pussy-88504.html.

Harris, Neil. *Humbug: The Art of P.T. Barnum*. Boston: Little Brown, 1973.

Heasley, Shaun. "Lady Gaga Wheelchair Act Raises Eyebrows." *Disability Scoop*. 15 July 2011. 2 June 2012.

Hebdige, Dick. *Subculture, the meaning of style*. London: Routledge, 1993.

Henderson, Carol E. "AKA: Sarah Baartman, The Hottentot Venus, and Black Women's Identity." *Women's Studies*, vol. 43, 2014, 946–959. *Literature Resource Center,* 27 April 2017.

Hooper, Tobe. "The Funhouse Retrospective: An Interview with Tobe Hooper." *Shock Till You Drop*. By Ryan Turek. 22 June 2010. 12 May 2012.

Juno, Andrea and V. Vale. *Bob Flanagan: Supermasochist*. People Series, Vol 1. Re/Search, 1993.

Kafer, Alison. "Desire and Disgust: My Ambivalent Adventures in Devoteeism." *Sex and Disability*, edited by Robert McRuer and Anna Mollow. Duke UP, 2012, pp. 331–354.

King, Stephen. "Why We Crave Horror Movies." *Playboy*. 1981. 13 May 2012.

Klause, Annette Curtis. *Freaks, Alive on the Inside!* New York: Simon Pulse, 2006.

Lady Gaga. "Bad Romance." *The Fame Monster*. Santa Monica: Interscope, 2009.

———. "Born This Way." *Born This Way*. Santa Monica: Interscope, 2011.

———. "Born This Way." Music Video. LadyGaga.Com. 5 June 2012.

———. "Dance in the Dark." *The Fame Monster*. Santa Monica: Interscope, 2010.

———. "Paparazzi." Music Video. LadyGaga.Com. 5 June 2012.

"Lady Gaga Bio." LadyGaga.Com. 29 May 2012.

Larsen, Nella. *Quicksand*. New Brunswick: Rutgers UP, 2008.

Larsen, R. and B. Haller. "The Case of Freaks." *Journal of Popular Film and Television*. 29.4 (Winter 2002): 164–172. EBSCOhost. 24 March 2011.

"Lesbian Amputee Little Arm Love." *Xvideos*. 16 May 2017. https://www.xvideos.com/video16091115/lesbian_amputee_little_arm_love#_tab Comments.

Lewis, Bradley. "A Mad Fight: Psychiatry and Disability Activism." *The Disability Studies Reader*, Edited by Lennard J. Davis, 4th Edition, Routledge, 2013, pp. 115–131.

Lindemann, Kurt. "Book & Film Reviews: *Murderball*." *Disability Studies Quarterly*. 26.2 (2006): n. pag. 21 August 2012.

Lindemann, Kurt and James L. Cherney. "Communicating In and Through 'Murderball': Masculinity and Disability in Wheelchair Rugby." *Western Journal of Communication* 72.2 (2008): 107–125. August 2012.

Lindfors, Bernth. "Ethnological Show Business: Footlighting the Dark Continent." *Freakery: Cultural Spectacles of the Extraordinary Body*. Edited by Rosemarie Garland-Thomson. NY UP, 1996. 207–218.

Mairs, Nancy. "Carnal Acts." *Staring Back: The Disability Experience from the Inside Out*. Ed. Kenny Fries. Plume: New York, 1997. 51–61.

"The Man Who Lost His Face." *TLC*. 2011.

"The Man with the 200 Pound Tumor." *TLC*. June 2012.

Marilyn Manson. "The Beautiful People." *Antichrist Superstar*. New Orleans: Nothing Records, 1996.

———. "The Beautiful People." *YouTube*. January 2012.

—————-. *Manson Wiki: The Marilyn Manson Encyclopedia.* 17 January 2013.

—————-. "mOBSCENE." *YouTube.* January 2012.

Marilyn Manson with Neil Strauss. *The Long Hard Road Out of Hell.* New York: Regan Books, 1998.

McNamara, Mary. "Review: 'Push Girls' captures a beautiful reality." *Los Angeles Times.* 4 June 2012. 30 June 2012.

McRuer, Robert. "Crip Eye for the Normate Guy: Queer Theory, Bob Flanagan, and the Disciplining of Disability Studies." *Cultural Front: Crip Theory: Cultural Signs of Queerness and Disability.* NYU Press, 2006. *ProQuest 24 April 2017.*

McRuer, Robert and Anna Mollow. "Introduction." *Sex and Disability.* Durham: Duke UP, 2012. 1–34.

Metz, Christian. *The Imaginary Signifier: Psychoanalysis and the Cinema.* Bloomington: Indiana UP, 1986.

Miller, Toby. *Television Studies, the Basics.* London: Routledge, 2010.

Moore, Ryan. *Sells Like Teen Spirit: Music Youth Culture and Social Crisis.* New York: New York UP, 2010.

Mulvey, Laura. "Visual Pleasure and Narrative Cinema." *Film Theory and Criticism: Introductory Readings.* Eds. Leo Braudy and Marshall Cohen. NY: Oxford UP, 1999: 833–844.

Murfett, Andrew. "Lady Gaga." "Lady Gaga." *Sydney Morning Herald.* 15 May 2009. 15 June 2012.

"My Story." *Zombie Boy.* http://rickgenest.com. 15 June 2012.

Negra, Diane. "Coveting the Feminine: Victor Frankenstein, Norman Bates, and Buffalo Bill." *Literature Film Quarterly.* (April 1996): 193–200. *EBSCOhost.* 15 March 2012.

Nichols, Bill. *Introduction to Documentary.* 2nd Ed. Bloomington: Indiana UP, 2010.

Nord, Derek. "Disability and Pornography." *Encyclopedia of Interpersonal Violence.* Edited by Claire M. Renzetti and Jeffrey L. Edleson, Vol. 1. Sage, 2008. 185–186.

Oates, Barb. "As real as it gets—Sundance Channel's 'Push Girls.'" *Channel Guide Magazine.* 1 June 2012. 30 June 2012.

"Our Mission." *Born This Way Foundation.* 15 January 2013.

Paglia, Camille. "Lady Gaga and the death of sex." *The Sunday Times.* 12 September 2010. *Sunday Times Magazine.* 1 June 2012.

Pearson, Lisa. "Engaging your superfans: Social lessons from Lady Gaga's manager." Bazaarvoice.blog. 25 June 2012. 15 January 2013.

Pfefferman, Naomi. "Women in wheelchairs push boundaries in real life and on TV." *The Times of Israel.* 11 June 2012. 30 June 2012.

Phillips, Kendall R. *Projected Fears: Horror Films and American Culture.* Westport: Praeger, 2005.

Pozner, Jennifer L. *Reality Bites Back: The Troubling Truth About Guilty Pleasure TV*. Berkeley: Seal Press, 2010.

Preira, Matt. "Marilyn Manson's *Antichrist Superstar* is 15: A Video Retrospective." *The Times*. 12 June 2012.

"Punk Amputee POV Fucked Doggystyle…" *Porn Hub*. 16 May 2017. https://www.pornhub.com/view_video.php?viewkey=ph58a08f6047531.

*Push Girls*. Sundance Channel. Season One. 2012.

"Breaking Back In." 1: 14. 27 August 2012.

"Breaking the Ice." 1: 11. 6 August 2012.

"Everyone Stares." E: 1. 4 June 2012.

"Fired Up." 1: 6. 2 July 2012.

"Freaky Deaky." 1: 9. 23 July 2012.

"How'd I Get Here?" 1: 5. 25 June 2012.

"How You Get Through." 1: 7. 9 July 2012.

"Living in the Fast Lane. 1: 8. 16 July 2012.

"Moving On," 1: 12. 13 August 2012.

"Watch Me." 1: 2. 4 June 2012.

"Quad Amputee Beauty." *Porn Hub*. 16 May 2017. https://www.pornhub.com/view_video.php?viewkey=ph58ac0d75b7112.

Reynolds, Dawn. "Disability and BDSM: Bob Flanagan and the Case for Sexual Rights." *Sexuality Research and Social Policy*, vol. 4, no. 1, March 2007, pp. 40–52.

Richardson, Niall. *Transgressive Bodies: Representations in Film and Popular Culture*. Routledge, 2016.

Robinson, Lisa. "Lady Gaga's Cultural Revolution." *Vanity Fair*. September 2010. VanityFair.com. 1 June 2012.

Rosen, Philip. "Text and Subject." *Narrative, Apparatus, Ideology*. NY: Columbia UP, 1986.

Russo, Mary. "Freaks." *The Horror Reader*. Ed. Ken Gelder. New York: Routledge, 2005. 90–96.

Savada, Elias. "The Making of Freaks: the events leading up to the creation of Tod Browning's classic." 2004. *Olga Baclanova*. Ed. Elias Savada. 2 February 2012.

Schaikewitz, Mia (@MiaSchaikewitz). "NEVER. If someone is ever inspired that is the most wonderful gift ever." Twitter.com. 27 July 2012, 3:05 a.m. 29 October 2012.

Schriempf, Alexa. "(Re)fusing the Amputated Body: An Interactionist Bridge for Feminism and Disability." *Hypatia*, vol. 16, no. 4, Fall 2001, pp. 53–79.

Sedgwick, Eve Kosofsky. *Epistemology of the Closet*. Berkeley: University of California Press, 2008.

Shapiro, Joseph P. "Tiny Tims, Supercrips, and the End of Pity." Shapiro, Joseph P. *No Pity: People with Disabilities Forging a New Civil Rights Movement*. New York: Three Rivers Press, 1994. 12–40.

Siebers, Tobin. *Disability Theory*. Ann Arbor: The University of Michegan Press, 2011.

———. "A Sexual Culture for Disabled People." *Sex and Disability*, edited by Robert McRuer and Anna Mollow. Duke UP, 2012, pp. 37–53.

Sprague, Erik. *Once More Through the Modified Looking Glass*. 2003–2009. Self-published.

Striker, Henri-Jacques. *A History of Disability*. Trns. Williams Sayers. Ann Arbor: The University of Michigan Press, 2002.

Sturken, Marita and Lisa Cartwright. *Practices of Looking: An Introduction to Visual Culture*. Oxford: Oxford UP, 2004.

*Sundance Channel*. "Frequently Asked Questions." 20 June 2013.

"Sundance Channel Greenlights New Original Non-Fiction Series 'Push Girls.'" *Press Releases. Sundance Channel*. 14 January 2012. 30 June 2012.

Switaj, Elizabeth Kate. "Lady Gaga's Bodies." *The Performance Identities of Lady Gaga*. Ed. Richard J. Gray II. Jefferson: McFarland & Co., 2012. 33–51.

Tibbles, J.A.R. "The Proteus Syndrome: The Elephant Man Diagnosed." 13 September 1986. *JSTOR*. 04 Feb 2012.

*TLC. A Discovery Company*. 3 September 2012.

Torrusio, Ann T. "The Fame Monster: The Monstrous Construction of Lady Gaga." *The Performance Identities of Lady Gaga*. Ed. Richard J. Gray II. Jefferson: McFarland & Co., 2012. 160–172.

"The Transcontinental Disability Choir: Disability Chic? (Temporary) Disability in Lady Gaga's 'Paparazzi.'" *Bitch Media*. 20 November 2009. 6 June 2012.

Turner, Matthew R. "Performing Pop: Lady Gaga, 'Weird Al' Yankovic and Parodied Performance." *The Performance Identities of Lady Gaga*. Ed. Richard J. Gray II. Jefferson: McFarland & Co., 2012. 188–202.

"The Vault" The Complete Marilyn Manson Archives." *The Nachtkabarett: Marilyn Manson, Art, and The Occult*. 21 June 2012.

Wiederhorn, Jon. "The Argument: Marilyn Manson is the only true artist today." *MTV*. 20 December 2013.

Williams, Linda. "Film Bodies: Gender, Genre, and Excess." *Film Quarterly*. vol. 44, no. 4, Summer 1991, pp. 2–13.

———. "Melodrama Revised." *Reconfiguring American Film Genres*. Ed. Nick Browne. Berkeley: University of California Press, 1998. 42–88.

———. "Power, Pleasure, and Perversion: Sadomasochistic Film Pornography." *Representations*. 27 (Summer 1989): 37–65. *JSTOR*. 2 June 2013.

———. "'Something Else Besides a Mother': *Stella Dallas* and the Maternal Melodrama." *Cinema Journal*. 24:1 (Autumn 1984): 2–27. *JSTOR*. 16 October 2013.

————. "When the Woman Looks." *The Dread of Difference: Gender and the Horror Film*. Ed. Barry Keith Grant. Austin: University of Texas Press, 1996. 15–24.

"The Year in Style: Lady Gaga." *The New York Times*. 24 December 2009. 31 May 2012.

Young, Stella. "Going Gaga Over Wheels." *Ramp Up*. 15 July 2011. 2 June 2012.

Zimmerman, David and Chet Cooper. "Push Girls: The Real Spokeswomen of LA." *Ability Magazine*. Aug/Sept, 2012. 30 June 2012.

# INDEX

© The Editor(s) (if applicable) and The Author(s) 2017      183

J.L. Williams, *Media, Performative Identity, and the New American Freak Show*, DOI 10.1007/978-3-319-66462-0